HTH.

Underground and Overground Trains

Capital Transport

nerson

This 1938 Tube Stock train, now in the ownership of the London Transport Museum, makes occasional appearances around the network on special pre-booked railtours. Similar trains remain in passenger service on the Isle of Wight (see Afterlife chapter). *Kim Rennie*

Title page Little and large at Kensal Green. A 1972 Tube Stock train is seen alongside a Class 378 of London Overground, the latter of similar loading gauge to the Underground's Large Profile trains. *Kim Rennie*

First published 2013
Reprinted 2013

ISBN 978 1 85414 364 8

Published by Capital Transport Publishing Ltd
www.capitaltransport.com

Printed by Parksons Graphics

CONTENTS

The cover photos are by Kim Rennie and show 1973 Tube Stock on the Piccadilly Line between Stamford Brook and Ravenscourt Park and Overground 378/2 stock at Olympia.

AUTHOR'S NOTE

This book describes and illustrates the rolling stock that runs on London's Underground and on the services operated by London Overground.

In the years since the last edition of London Underground Rolling Stock, this book's predecessor, much has changed. The Waterloo & City Line was upgraded in 2006, adding 25% more capacity, with passengers benefiting from a smoother ride, enhanced reliability and reduced journey times. A seventh carriage was added to all Jubilee Line trains from late 2005 and early 2006, providing around 17% more capacity, which has already been absorbed by the increase in demand accompanying passenger growth at Canary Wharf. At the time of compilation all of the Victoria Line's new trains were in passenger service, whilst all but one of the new air-conditioned trains were running on the Metropolitan Line. A full refurbishment of the existing fleet of District Line trains was completed in 2008; over the next few years, new air conditioned trains will serve the line. What is now known as London Overground passed into Transport for London (TfL) hands in late 2007. New trains ordered by the new administration came into service progressively from 2009.

New rolling stock is a key component of the massive major upgrade plan for the London Underground and Overground currently underway. In a move stated to be the largest rail system upgrade in the world nearly two thousand new coaches are being supplied to London Underground. Notably the Metropolitan, District, Circle and Hammersmith & City Lines will gain a single fleet of increased size to replace the 177 trains of differing types used before renewal. These trains have faster acceleration than previous types and also have regenerative braking, which returns around 20 per cent of the electricity used to the supply network.

Thanks are given to all who have contributed and offered advice, particularly Brian Hardy, Transport for London, the London Transport Museum, photographic contributors and many others.

The London Underground Railway Society (lurs.org.uk) publishes regular rolling stock information in its monthly magazine *Underground News*, to enable its members to keep the information in this book (correct to 9 December 2012) up to date.

ABBREVIATIONS

Abbreviations used for car builders:

ABB ABB Transportation (later ADtranz), Derby. Now Bombardier Transportation UK.

BREL BREL Ltd, Derby (later became ABB Transportation Ltd).

Birmingham Birmingham Railway Carriage & Wagon Company Ltd.

Bombardier Bombardier Prorail Ltd, Horbury, Wakefield. Now Bombardier Transportation UK.

Cravens Cravens Ltd, Sheffield.

Derby British Railways Workshops, Derby.

Gloucester Gloucester Railway Carriage & Wagon Company Ltd.

Metro-Cammell Metropolitan-Cammell Carriage & Wagon Company Ltd, Birmingham. Now Alstom.

RFS RFS Industries, Doncaster. Now Bombardier Transportation UK.

Other Abbreviations used:

AC	Alternating current
ATO	Automatic Train Operation
ATP	Automatic Train Protection
BRML	British Rail Maintenance Ltd
CDU	Cab Display Unit
CSDE	Correct Side Door Enable
CCTV	Closed Circuit Television
DC	Direct current
DMU	Diesel Multiple Unit
DMSO	Driving Motor Second Open
DVA	Digitised Voice Announcer
EMU	Electrical multiple unit
ETT	Experimental Tube Train
ERU	Emergency Response Unit
GEC	General Electric Company
IGBT	See Appendix at end of book
JLE	Jubilee Line Extension
LED	Light emitting diode
LOROL	London Overground Rail Operations Ltd
LT	London Transport
LUL	London Underground Limited
MSO	Motor Second Open
NDM	Non-driving motor car
NSE	Network SouthEast
OPO	One-person operation
PLS	Programme Logic System
PPP	Public Private Partnership
PTSO	Pantograph Trailer Second Open
SCAT	Speed Control After Tripping
T	Trailer
TBTC	Transmission-based train control
TEP	Train Equipment Panel
TfL	Transport for London
TMS	Train Monitoring System
TSO	Trailer Second Open
UNDM	Uncoupling Non-Driving Motor Car

INTRODUCTION

London Underground Ltd operates two main types of passenger rolling stock on its railways. One is known as surface, sub-surface or large-profile stock and is built to full-size loading gauge for use on the Metropolitan, Circle, Hammersmith & City and District lines, whose tunnel sections are double-tracked and run just below surface level. The trains of London Overground share this same profile.

The other type, known as tube stock, is used on the Bakerloo, Piccadilly, Northern, Jubilee, Central, Victoria and Waterloo & City lines, which have deep-level single-track tunnels of about 12ft diameter. The tube tunnels on the Jubilee Line extension east of Green Park, however, have been built to a diameter of 14 feet.

In the case of tube stock, the different groups are distinguished by the year of anticipated delivery at the time of ordering. Surface stock is distinguished by letters and optionally a single digit suffix indicating the number of cars forming the train (previously the suffix indicated the last two digits of the year of anticipated delivery; for instance the District Line stock officially known as D Stock, was originally designated D78 Stock).

Each train is composed of one or more units coupled together as necessary to form trains of the required length. Units are formed of a number of motor cars and trailer cars semi-permanently coupled. Each unit is self-sufficient as regards current supply for motors, lighting, compressed air supply and auxiliary equipment. Some stocks have units which cannot be operated in service on their own, as they have a driver's cab at one end only, with a shunting control panel at the other. The Central Line's 1992 Tube Stock also has some units which have a shunting control panel at each end and these will always be formed in the middle of trains.

The different types of car are:

DM   Driving Motor car, having traction motors and a driver's cab.

NDM Non-Driving Motor car – as DM but without a driver's cab.

UNDM Uncoupling Non-Driving Motor car – as NDM but provided with control cabinet at one end to allow uncoupling and shunting of a unit without loss of space incurred by the cab.

T   Trailer car – without motors or cab.

S7 and S8 trains contain an MS (Motor Shunting) car described on page 21.

To assist in identification, the end cars of units are referred to as 'A' cars (which normally face north or west) or 'D' cars (south or east). Car numbering is also arranged so that distinction can not only be made between 'A' and 'D' cars but also between the types of car and stock. To simplify shunting operations in Stonebridge

Park depot, the arrangements on the Bakerloo Line are opposite to that just described. It should be noted, however, that on lines that have loops at terminal stations (Kennington on the Northern Line and Heathrow on the Piccadilly Line) or have triangular junction layouts (for example Rickmansworth – Croxley – Moor Park on the Metropolitan Line), trains will become turned and may face the opposite direction to that mentioned above. The trains on the Central Line, however, are fully reversible and are not identified with the 'A' and 'D' nomenclature. A similar principle has been applied to the Northern Line's 1995 Tube Stock.

All trains on the Underground are now one-person operated. The 1972, 1973, C and D stocks were built as crew-operated trains and converted for opo later.

London Underground trains operate on the fourth-rail system at 630V DC, although on some lines the line voltage will be raised to 750V. On London Overground routes the electric trains operate on the third-rail system at 750V DC and from overhead lines at 25kV AC. There are also a small number of diesel trains.

Trains tend to average a speed of around 20 mph (33 km/h), a figure that takes account of station stops. The upper limit in central London is 30 to 40 mph (48 to 64 km/h), on account of the short distances between stations, except on the Victoria Line, where stations are further apart. Here trains can reach up to 50 mph (80 km/h). On the outer stretches of the Metropolitan Line, trains can reach over 60 mph (96 km/h).

According to Transport for London (TfL) most rolling stock lasts around 40 years. Major refurbishment can prolong life by another 10-15 years and costs around a sixth of the cost of a new train. The longest lived trains of recent times were the Metropolitan Line's A Stock, which was initially introduced in 1961 and was in passenger service for more than 50 years.

Most surface and tube stock tends to remain on the line for which it was originally procured. The constraints are often physical. Not all tube lines have the same tunnel diameter. The original City & South London Railway tunnels were 10ft 2in (3.1 metres) in diameter. On lines built subsequently the internal tunnel diameters rose to 3.6 metres, up to 3.8 metres with the Victoria Line and 4.35m on new-build tunnels of the Jubilee Line extension. Other considerations include track curvature, signalling systems and platform length vis-à-vis train length also mean that rolling stock can usually only be used on one specific line. Notwithstanding these constraints stock transfers do take place when appropriate, such as when the 1983 stock introduced to the Jubilee line displaced 1972 Stock to the Northern Line. Northern Line 1959 Stock was then 'cascaded' to the Bakerloo Line.

Three types of large-profile train operate on London Underground – known as C, D and S Stock. The C and D Stock will be replaced progressively by the newer S7 and S8 Stock as part of London Underground's current operation to update its entire fleet of these trains using a standard design of rolling stock by 2015. The 50-year old A Stock on the Metropolitan Line was the first to be replaced, followed by the C Stock (Circle and Hammersmith & City lines), and finally the D Stock on the District Line. The new trains have an auto-close system for the doors, whereby they close automatically after 45 seconds to keep the air conditioning effective. They can then be reopened by a passenger so long as the Train Operator has not closed the doors for departure. *Capital Transport*

UNDERGROUND LARGE-PROFILE TRAINS
Metropolitan, District, Circle and Hammersmith & City Lines

C STOCK

C (Circle Line) Stock exists in two virtually identical variants. The first sub-type built was the C69 Stock that was introduced on the Circle and Hammersmith & City lines, the first train entering service in September 1970. These trains were followed by a batch of similar design (C77) for the Edgware Road to Wimbledon branch of the District Line where short platforms on the western part of the Circle Line preclude the use of the longer District Line D Stock cars. The C77 Stock entered service from December 1977. Both batches were built by Metro-Cammell of Birmingham. The first batch, comprising 212 cars made up of 35 six-car trains and one spare two-car unit, was ordered in 1968. The second batch comprised 67 cars for 11 trains. Refurbishment took place between 1991 and 1994 by RFS Industries of Doncaster.

The design parameters of these trains took specific regard of frequent stops and short intervals between stations, also high passenger density and the need to move people on and off trains rapidly. New technical features included a secondary suspension system, thermostat controlled blower-heater fans mounted in the roofs and door vestibules affording increased standing space. The C Stock was also the first manually controlled stock on London Underground to be fitted with rheostatic braking (see Appendix), using the traction motors for braking. Another first was the 'selective close' facility, which in cold weather allowed all the doors except one pair to be closed to retain heat, while the trains were standing at terminal stations. Four pairs of double doors are fitted on each side of the cars.

Originally C Stock cars had internally illuminated advertisement frames, fitted high on the draught screens either side of the doorways. This feature was borrowed from the 1967 Tube Stock for generating additional advertising revenue. Unfortunately the cost of changing advertisements and general maintenance absorbed most of the additional income and the displays were removed when the cars were refurbished.

The seating was originally transverse except at the outer ends of the cars, which had longitudinal seats, but following refurbishment all seating is longitudinal throughout. Although the total number of seats remained unchanged, the new arrangement provided for additional standing room in the gangways. Windows were introduced in the car ends to enhance passenger security. In autumn 1997 work began fitting digital voice announcement (DVA) equipment to trains and four years later trains were given brighter, deeper and more comfortable seats.

C Stock trains are made up of two-car units of motor (M) and trailer (T) cars coupled semi-permanently. These in turn are marshalled into six-car trains, formed either as M–T+T–M+T–M or M–T+M–T+T–M.

	DM	T
Length per car	16.03m	14.94m
Width	2.92m	2.92m
Height	3.68m	3.68m
Weight	31.70 tonnes	20.2 tonnes
Seating per car	32	
Seating capacity per train	192	
Standing capacity per train	547	
Total six-car train capacity	739 *(based on 4 passengers per square metre)*	

Above C Stock trailer cars 6734 and 6606 are new-build replacements for two cars destroyed in the 7 July 2005 London bombings. In addition, 6548 was given major repairs. These were built by Bombardier at Dunakeszi in Hungary. Visible at the right-hand end of the coach is the 'inter-car barrier' devised and supplied by Creactive Designs to prevent passengers from falling into the gap between carriages. *Kim Rennie*

Opposite The bright interior of refurbished C Stock was a big improvement on the original claustrophobic layout, albeit involving the sacrifice of the transverse seating in line with the modern policy of maximising standing room. *Capital Transport*

D STOCK

D (for District Line) Stock (also termed D78 Stock) runs on all sections of the District Line except between Edgware Road and High Street Kensington. The fleet of 75 aluminium-bodied six-car trains was introduced in stages between 1980 and 1983. Originally manufactured by Metro-Cammell in Birmingham, the trains were refurbished between 2006 and 2008 by Bombardier Transportation UK in Derby.

Each train is composed of two separate three-car units, made up of driving motor cars (DM) fitted with driver's controls and traction motors, uncoupling non-driving motor cars (UNDM) fitted with traction/control equipment plus a small cabinet allowing uncoupling and shunting (but without full driver's controls or cab) and trailer coaches (T) that have no driving controls or traction equipment. The trains are similar in length to the older seven-car trains they replaced, each D Stock car

A train of D Stock runs alongside the overhead-wire electrified London Tilbury and Southend line at West Ham. D Stock shared with the now-withdrawn 1983 Tube Stock single-leaf doors and is now unique on the Underground in having these. *Kim Rennie*

being longer to compensate. In this way the number of wheelsets per train was decreased, reducing maintenance costs. The aluminium construction makes the trains lighter, lessening train noise and vibration.

The D78 Stock shares many design similarities with the 1973 Tube Stock that runs on the Piccadilly Line, particularly in its traction package and wheels, which are of the smaller tube-train size. Most surface stock has 3ft 6in (1,067mm wheels), the traditional size for main line carriages, whereas tube stock has 2ft 7in (790mm) wheels. The use of smaller wheels allows lower floors and thus greater headroom for passengers. It was also envisaged that maintenance costs could be reduced by reducing the different types of wheels and bogies in use.

Opening quarter-light windows and concealed fans in the ceilings provide a comfortable level of ventilation (the fans and opening windows were not part of the original design and were retrofitted after the trains were delivered). Seating is mostly longitudinal with a double pair of transverse seats in the centre of each car. A departure from normal design was the door arrangement, with four pairs of single leaf doors per side in each car. These doors have proved a major hindrance in the rush hour and have not been repeated on newer designs of Underground train.

Traction brake controls comprise a right-hand 'fore and aft' vertical lever incorporating the 'dead man' device, instead of the previous left-hand rotary operated controller.

Refurbishment of the trains took place between 2006 and 2008. Externally the stock was painted in London Underground colours, whilst the interiors underwent a complete refresh, including car end windows and CCTV added to increase security. Significant improvements to the passenger information system were made with saloon dot-matrix station/destination displays and new equipment for digital voice announcements. Accessibility for passengers was improved, with features such as tip-up seats to accommodate wheelchairs, buggies and luggage.

	DM	UNDM	T
Length per car	18.37m	18.12m	18.12m
Width	2.85m	2.85m	2.85m
Height	3.62m	3.62m	3.62m
Weight	27.46 tonnes	26.11 tonnes	18.40 tonnes
Seating	44	48	48
Seating capacity per train	280		
Standing capacity per train	547		
Train capacity, six cars	827 *(based on 4 passengers per square metre)*		

Between Ravenscourt Park and Turnham Green District Line trains such as this D Stock example run above street level on lines belonging once to the London & South Western Railway. This service began in June 1877 and provides convenient access to the District's Richmond and Ealing Broadway branches. *Kim Rennie*

D Stock interior. The narrow doors create a bottleneck when trains are busy and will not be replicated on newer designs of train. *Kim Rennie*

S7 AND S8 STOCK

S Stock is the new type of train being introduced to replace trains on all the surface and sub surface lines and exists in two variants, S7 and S8. S7 is a seven-car version for the Circle, Hammersmith & City and District Lines, whilst the eight-car version (S8) works only on the Metropolitan Line. Both variants share common design characteristics and specifications but they diverge in particular details that reflect the differing characters of the lines that they serve. The Circle Line, for instance, is characterised by dense, short-distance ridership which is best handled by trains with fewer seats and more standing room. Passengers on the Uxbridge, Watford and Amersham services of the Metropolitan Line expect a higher proportion of seats on their longer journeys and at least some transverse seating (the A stock it replaced had 100% transverse seating).

A Metropolitan Line train of S8 Stock a Neasden. The blue lamp next to the starting signal on the left is part of the new signalling system on the Jubilee Line. *Kim Rennie*

The new fleet will eventually number 191 trains or 1,395 cars of standardised car design. According to the manufacturer, Bombardier Transportation UK, the S Stock order is the largest single order of rolling stock ever made in the history of the railways in Britain. Built at Derby, the S Stock trains embody several innovations. They are the first London Underground trains with air conditioning, which is duplicated so that 50 per cent capacity still remains available if one system fails. Full-width gangways between coaches create a sense of openness and security, also providing extra room for standing passengers. The inside of the train is thus one continuous saloon, providing improved capacity, security and passenger flow.

After a period of trial running in Monday to Friday off-peaks, S7 stock entered daily service on the Hammersmith & City Line from 9th December 2012. This view is at West Ham. *Kim Rennie*

Closed-circuit television (CCTV) enables the driver to watch every car when the train is stationary, with additional cameras providing a view of the whole of the outside of the train, to ensure passenger safety before the train leaves a station. On-train information is improved too. Automated voice announcements are provided and the electronic displays are larger than previously, using clearer lettering that avoids the coarse dot-matrix appearance of older electronic displays. The indicators show the train's destination and the line; they can also display other messages, such as safety notices. Indicators are also provided externally and on the longer distance trains the displays alternate between destination, stopping pattern and line name, e.g. Amersham, All Stations, and Metropolitan Line.

Every axle of the train is motored, maximising acceleration rates and also improving braking capability. As with the 2009 Tube Stock, the doors are electrically operated, although on the S Stock the doors are screw-driven instead of arm-operated. The doors have obstacle detection and sensitive edges.

Traction is provided by AC asynchronous electric motors driven using Insulated Gate Bipolar Transistor (IGBT) controllers (see Appendix) and the DC 630V supply and the train is capable of regenerative braking (see Appendix) at 790V. In due course, power upgrades will increase the line voltage to 750V allowing regenerative braking at 890V. This significantly improves the energy efficiency of the trains. Braking is controlled by the latest technology, the Knorr Bremse EP2002 system, which employs data bus links along the train to improve brake effectiveness taking into account a wide range of parameters.

The S Stock uses the same tripcock train protection system traditionally used by London Underground, although it is planned to upgrade this by 2018, installing Bombardier's own CityFlow 650 signalling system in readiness for driverless or unattended train operation (see Appendix) and protection.

The very generous provision for wheelchairs in the S7 Stock also provides the potential for a big increase in standing capacity in the peak hours, subject of course to those using the tip-up seats being willing to stand up. *Capital Transport*

The first line to receive the new S Stock trains was the Metropolitan (in August 2010), enabling the A Stock to be replaced. Roll-out is following on the Hammersmith & City Line, then the Circle Line and finally the District, with the whole programme scheduled for completion in 2016.

S7 TRAINS	DM	M1	M2	MS
Length per car	17.44m	15.43m	15.43m	15.43m
Width	2.92m	2.92m	2.92m	2.92m
Height	2.88m	2.88m	2.88m	2.88m
Weight	33.45 tonnes	30.44 tonnes	27.45 tonnes	29.20 tonnes
Per train	213.7 tonnes			

Total seating capacity 256 with another 24 tip-up seats and four wheelchair spaces (or an additional 14 tip-up seats).
Total standing capacity 609
Total passenger capacity 865 (based on 4 passengers per square metre)

S8 TRAINS	DM	M1	M2	MS
Length per car	17.44m	15.43m	15.43m	15.43m
Width	2.92m	2.92m	2.92m	2.92m
Height	2.88m	2.88m	2.88m	2.88m
Weight	33.64 tonnes	30.63 tonnes	27.64 tonnes	29.33 tonnes
Per train	242.56 tonnes			

Total seating capacity 306 with another 36 tip-up seats and four wheelchair spaces (or an additional 14 tip-up seats).
Total standing capacity 697
Total passenger capacity 1,003 (based on 4 passengers per square metre)

The cars shown as types M1, M2 and MS are all non-driving motors. Type M1 is a conventional non-driving motor car and included in all train formations. M2 cars are not essential components. It is understood that originally it was intended that the C-stock would be replaced by trains containing no M2 cars but it was decided subsequently that all trains would have at least one M2 car, with 8-car trains including two. The middle cars are Motor Shunting (MS) cars, which are fitted with semi-permanent couplings so that trains can be separated and driven at depots.

Three trains of S7 layout have been temporarily formed into eight-car formation for use on the Metropolitan Line (see Unit Formations). When these trains revert to S7 formation, M2 cars 25382, 25384 and 25386 will each be incorporated into a new build train.

The roomy look of the S7 Stock for the Circle, Hammersmith & City and Edgware Road to Wimbledon services. The wider and full-length gangway makes it easier to pass through the train and creates a sense of openness and security. S Stock is the first air-conditioned stock on the Underground. *Capital Transport*

The Metropolitan Line's S8 Stock has some transverse seating, reflecting the longer average journeys made on this line and the unsuitability of longitudinal seats for such journeys. Straphangers were retrofitted to S8 stock soon after all had entered service. *Capital Transport*

A 1996 Tube Stock train on the Jubilee Line is passed by an S8 Stock train on the fast tracks between Finchley Road and Wembley Park.
Kim Rennie

UNDERGROUND TUBE TRAINS

Northern, Central, Bakerloo, Piccadilly, Victoria and Jubilee Lines

A 1972 Tube Stock Bakerloo Line train bound for Elephant & Castle heads south at Harlesden on the so-called DC Lines which run parallel to the West Coast Main Line. The DC lines are shared with London Overground trains from Euston to Watford Junction.
Kim Rennie

1972 STOCK (Bakerloo Line)

The design of the 1972 Stock, all remaining units of which work on the Bakerloo Line, was virtually identical to that of the 1967 Stock (now all withdrawn) for the Victoria Line, but was built for crew operation rather than automatic operation with a single man crew and is formed of seven car trains rather than ones of eight cars. Thirty of these trains were built for use on the Northern Line by Metro-Cammell at Birmingham. The initial order comprised 90 driving motor cars, 90 trailers and 30 uncoupling non-driving motor cars, all in unpainted aluminium. The trains were formed into three- and four-car units, one of each being required to form a complete train (M–T–T–M+UNDM–T–M). The first train entered service on the Northern Line on 26 June 1972 and all 30 were in service by June 1973. Some of these cars were later converted to run on the Victoria Line, whilst others were converted to one-person operation for the Bakerloo Line.

The second batch of 1972 Tube Stock (1972 MkII) was intended for eventual use on what became the Jubilee Line but saw service first on the Northern Line (replacing 1938 Tube Stock there). The 1972 MkII order for 33 trains, placed also with Metro-Cammell, comprised 99 driving motor cars, 99 trailers and 33 uncoupling non-driving motor cars. The first trains entered service in November 1973, generally similar in appearance its MkI predecessors but with cosmetic changes such as repositioned train number plates, red-painted passenger doors and the Underground roundel on carriage sides instead of the word Underground. The MkII trains were also fitted with 'calling on lights' as introduced on 1967 stock and although the MkI and MkII trains were not compatible when delivered, subsequent modifications enabled them to be coupled and run together.

From 1977 trains of 1972 MkII Stock, displaced by the 1959 Stock on the Northern Line, began working on the Bakerloo Line in readiness for the Stanmore branch becoming the Jubilee Line (in 1979). The transfer process was a gradual one, completed in time for the opening of the Jubilee Line between Stanmore and Charing Cross on 1 May 1979. In the interim period, the 1972 MkII Stock worked on the Bakerloo Line, including to and from Watford Junction. Four MkII trains were returned to the Northern Line during 1983 and subsequently a further 14 trains followed them in 1984 and 1985. The delivery of new stock for the Jubilee allowed the 1972 MkII Stock on that line to be transferred to the Bakerloo, which was achieved in March 1989. OPO on the Bakerloo Line commenced on 20 November 1989 after the stock had been converted at Acton Works. Refurbishment by Tickford Rail took place at Rosyth Royal Dockyard between 1991 and 1995.

The majority of MkI trains are no longer in service, though 26 cars remain in service on the Bakerloo Line together with most MkII trains.

	DM	UNDM	T
Length per car	16.09m	15.98m	15.98m
Width	2.642m	2.642m	2.642m
Height	2.87m	2.87m	2.87m
Weight			
MkI	28.2 tons	26.8 tons	18.6 tons
MkII	27.8 tons	26.5 tons	18.1 tons
Seating	40	40	36
Total seating capacity	268		
Total standing capacity	466		
Total seven-car train capacity	734 (*based on 4 passengers per square metre*)		

Above Northbound 1972 Stock train at Queens Park station. The blue solid circle following the car number signifies that this unit is fitted with deicing equipment. South of this point the Bakerloo Line dives into tube tunnels, whereas the London Overground trains diverge to run to Euston. *Capital Transport*

Right Interior of a refurbished 1972 Stock trailer. *Capital Transport*

Additional length and subtle differences in design details distinguish the exterior of the 1973 Stock of the Piccadilly Line from its Bakerloo Line cousins. This train is at Oakwood, one of the 1930s stations designed by Charles Holden. *Brian Hardy*

Opposite A 1973 Stock train at Turnham Green, with a double-ended unit nearest the camera (the inter-car barrier fixings give the clue). *Kim Rennie*

Opposite lower The appearance of a normal Driving Motor car. *Capital Transport*

1973 STOCK

When extension of the Piccadilly Line to Heathrow Airport was being planned it was clear that new, purpose-built trains with additional space for luggage would be extremely desirable. For this reason an order was placed with Metro-Cammell of Birmingham for 87½ six-car trains (525 cars) comprising 196 driving motor cars, 175 trailers and 154 uncoupling non-driving motor cars. Each car was built about six feet longer than cars of earlier stock but the total length of a 6-car train was about 17 feet shorter than a seven-car 1956/59 Tube Stock train. This enabled the complete train to fit into the platforms at all tube stations on the line, which was necessary because the stock was subsequently converted to one-person operation, which was the intention when it was built. The first train of 1973 Tube Stock entered service on 19 July 1975 in the form of a passenger-carrying 'special' for the opening to Hatton Cross, followed on 15 August 1975 by the first normal passenger working.

The majority of trains operate in the formation M–T–UNDM+UNDM–T–M. The driving motor cars at each end were provided with mechanical couplers only, whereas the UNDM cars in the middle positions were fitted with automatic couplers. In addition there were 21 three-car units formed M–T–M known as 'double-cab' units, with automatic couplers on each driving motor car. The purpose of these latter units was to give fleet flexibility, being able to replace a normal single end unit requiring maintenance. One unit was also provided to operate the Holborn–Aldwych shuttle service, which continued until its closure on 30 September 1994.

Improvements incorporated in these trains included provision of air-operated cab doors, operated independently of the passenger doors, and a 'selective door close' facility enabling all except one single door and one single leaf of a double door on each car to be closed, a useful facility in bad weather at terminal stations and during prolonged station stops. After trials on a 1967 Tube Stock unit, the Westcode electro-pneumatic braking system was provided, enabling the Westinghouse air brake to be omitted. A train equipment fault-finding panel was provided in the cab for the driver to identify faults on the train. Also provided was automatic wheel-slip/slide protection and load control of acceleration and braking.

On all 1973 Stock cars, the interior seating was arranged longitudinally at each end of the saloon, with transverse seats in the centre section bay, each type of car having seats for 44 passengers. Sliding ventilators were provided above the car windows. The intention to fit three ceiling-mounted fans on each car was hampered by design and technical difficulties and it was not until October 1977 that fans were first used. Even so they were not wholly successful. Not all cars were fitted with fans and those that did have them were subsequently decommissioned. A total of 25 single-ended A' units were fitted from new with de-icing equipment.

The Piccadilly Line was the first of the deep-level tube lines to be converted to one-person operation, as of 31 August 1987. The 1973 Stock was converted for OPO during 1986 and up to September 1987. The exterior differences included the fitting of an offside window wiper and calling-on light.

Following trials a contract for refurbishing the 1973 Stock was awarded to RFS, soon absorbed into Bombardier Prorail, with work commencing in May 1993. In the process grab rails were added for help with detraining, lighting provided above the driver's side cab window and additional lighting fitted at solebar level for use in emergencies. Internally all seating became longitudinal, reducing capacity from 44 to 38 per car. However, perch seats were provided at the car ends and by the door area in the centre bay, greatly enhancing luggage and standing space. Interior dot matrix indicators were provided and pre-set digital voice announcements became available, set up by the train operator. The first refurbished train re-entered service on 17 June 1996, the refurbishment programme continuing for four years.

The Piccadilly Line fleet now comprises 518 cars out of an original total of 525. Six have been scrapped (DMs 204 and 888, trailer 604 and UNDMs 314 and 404), while trailer 514 is now a track recording car in the engineering train fleet and DM 166 was damaged in the terrorist attack of 7 July 2005 and was subsequently scrapped.

	DM	UNDM	T
Length per car	17.48m	17.48m	17.48m
Width	2.63m	2.63m	2.63m
Height	2.88m	2.88m	2.88m
Weight	27.2 tonnes	26.2 tonnes	18.4 tonnes
Seating	38	38	38
Total seating capacity for six cars	228, plus 44 perch seats		
Total standing capacity for six cars	456		
Total six-car train capacity	684 *(based on 4 passengers per square metre)*		

Right Disfigured 1973 Stock car at Barons Court. The dark markings indicate a less than successful attempt to remove graffiti. The current policy of removing embellished trains from service means that the attacker's handiwork is no longer seen. Fortunately, CCTV surveillance and active security patrols are making it ever harder to disfigure tube trains. *Capital Transport*

Below 1973 Stock carriage interior. *Kim Rennie*

1992 STOCK (Central and Waterloo & City Lines)

Following trials with prototype trains, an order for 85 trains of Central Line Replacement Stock (as it was then known, now classified 1992 Tube Stock) was placed in 1989 with BREL of Derby, which through a succession of new owners has become Bombardier Transportation UK. The outcome was a fleet of modern trains incorporating a number of features such as electronic traction control and a fully integrated train control and management system.

Each train of 1992 Stock comprises eight cars formed of four two-car units. There are three combinations of 2-car unit and four types of individual vehicle. Car 'A' is a driving motor with cab, collector shoes, traction equipment and automatic coupler. Car 'B' is a non-driving motor car having no cab or shoes, but has traction equipment which is fed from the adjacent motor car. It also has a shunting control cabinet at its outer end along with an automatic coupler. Car type 'C' is similarly a non-driving motor car having no cab, but has shoes and traction equipment as an 'A' car, along with a shunting control cabinet and automatic coupler at its outer end. De-icing cars are a variation on car type 'C' and are designated as type 'D'. With these four types of car, semi-permanent two-car units are formed as follows: 175 A-B units, 133 B-C units and 32 B-D de-icing units. All the two-car units are fully reversible and compatible and thus there is no distinction between 'A' and 'D' ends as before. With the different combination of cars and units, it is possible for an 8-car train to be formed in one of 36 different ways, although DM cars are kept at the outer ends of trains whenever possible.

At Bank, one end of the short line from Waterloo, is a 1992 Stock Waterloo & City Line train. When first introduced these trains wore the blue, white and red livery of British's Rail's Network South East, who owned the line at the time. *Kim Rennie*

The body shells are made from welded extruded aluminium sections. The twin sliding doors, plus one single door at each end of each car, are wider than any used previously on tube stock. Each car has all-longitudinal seating, arranged six per side in the outer bays and five per side in the centre saloon bay (i.e. between the double doors), giving a total of 34 seats per car. The middle pair of each group of six is set back six inches to allow greater standing capacity, at which point there is a floor-to-ceiling grab pole in the centre. At non-cabbed ends (at the trailing end of car 'A' and both ends of cars 'B', 'C' and 'D') there is one perch seat in each corner position. The large single-glazed car windows, which curve up into the roof line, have also been adopted from the prototype trains. The passenger door width is 1,664mm (double) and 832mm (single) to allow speedier alighting and boarding and thereby reduce station stop times. The sliding doors are externally hung. Passenger door control buttons were provided from new. Since early 2000, however, the train doors have been under control of the train operator on this and all stocks fitted with such equipment. Apart from the driving end of the 'A' cars, end windows are provided to give greater security.

Other interior features include pre-programmed announcements in digitised speech. The driver's cab incorporates in-cab closed circuit television, which provides pictures of the relevant station platform, including views on departure. In addition to public address, in the event of an emergency, there is two-way communication between the driver and passengers. The driver has a redesigned fore/aft traction brake controller, which is positioned on the right hand of the driver's seat — reminiscent of that provided on the 1935 streamlined tube stock!

The thyristor controlled traction equipment is provided by a consortium of ASEA Brown Boveri of Switzerland and Brush Electrical Machines of Loughborough. A computer data transmission system with multiplexing is used for much of the electrical control of the trains. This reduces the number of cables, but safety-critical circuits such as braking are separately wired as well. The Westinghouse analogue braking system is fitted, along with air suspension. The bogies were originally provided by Kawasaki Heavy Industries of Osaka, Japan. Each car has six ventilation units giving full forced ventilation. The length of each car is 16,248mm over body ends, 2,620mm wide over door leaves and 2,869mm high at the top of the car roof.

Construction of the new Central Line trains began in the late-summer of 1990 and the first four-car train to be delivered arrived at Ruislip depot on 17 May 1992. The first train entered passenger service on the Central Line on 7 April 1993. This introduced one-person operation and Correct Side Door Enable (CSDE) on the Central

Line for the first time. With only two trains outstanding to be delivered, sufficient were available for the full Monday to Friday service to be worked with new trains from Monday 20 February 1995. The first stage of Automatic Train Protection commenced on the western branches to North Acton on 19 June 1995, where trains changed between ATP and tripcock modes. By 10 November 1997 the whole of the Central Line had been converted to ATP.

Replacement rolling stock was also required for the Waterloo & City Line, which was soldiering on with trains introduced in 1940. There were replaced in 1993 by new Class 482 trains that were virtually identical to 1992 Stock other than the Waterloo & City trains are not fitted with Automatic Train Control equipment. The fleet comprised ten two-car units that were an 'add-on' order to London Underground's 85 eight-car trains. Four-car trains are the rule on the Waterloo & City composed of two two-car sets, each formed of an 'E' DM and an 'F' NDM that are, in most respects, almost identical to the A-B two-car units on the Central Line. Being then owned by Network SouthEast, the only main visible difference was that the W&C trains were finished in a variation of the NSE livery — predominantly blue and white with a thin red line at floor level.

Timetabled 'ghost' running started on 12 July 1993 and passengers were carried on the modernised Waterloo & City Line from Monday 19 July 1993, all units being in service at some time during that day. The following year, on 1 April, the operation of the Waterloo & City Line was taken over by London Underground.

From 8 July 1996, 'Correct Side Door Enable' equipment was commissioned on the line. This equipment, also operational on the Central Line, is designed to prevent train operators opening passenger doors on the wrong side of the trains at stations. The trains underwent a mid-life overhaul and repainting into London Underground livery in 2006 as part of the refurbishment programme, when the Waterloo & City Line was closed from 1 April to 11 September.

	DM	NDM
Length per car	16.25m	16.25m
Width	2.62m	2.62m
Height	2.87m	2.87m
Weight	22.5 tonnes	20.5 tonnes
Seating	34	34
Total seating capacity for an eight-car train	272	
Total standing capacity for an eight-car train	620	
Total capacity for an eight-car train	892	

General view of 1992 Stock recently refreshed with new seating moquette and minor modifications.
Kim Rennie

This branding in the moquette covering of a priority seat is a welcome touch for those less able to stand for long periods.
Capital Transport

Opposite Refurbished Waterloo & City Line car interior, showing the arm rests fitted and differences in the seating layout.
Kim Rennie

1995 AND 1996 STOCK

In appearance the 1995 and 1996 Tube Stocks are almost identical to each other but equipment differences exist between each type. For this reason they are described separately. Both designs of train were future-proofed, in that they were capable of being retrofitted for Automatic Train Protection and Automatic Train Operation (see Appendix) at a later date. This was in fact implemented on the 1996 Stock trains used on the Jubilee Line, where the train follows instructions given by the on-train computer. Currently the 1995 Stock trains on the Northern Line are driven conventionally by train operators but conversion of this line to automatic operation is planned.

The inward-sloping sides and distinctive front window shapes, lamp clusters and grey paint treatment of the 1995 Stock constructed for the Northern Line demonstrate little in common with its counterparts built three years earlier. This view is at West Finchley.
Capital Transport

Much of the Edgware branch of the Northern Line forms a continuous green corridor, with dense undergrowth on either side. In this midwinter view, a 1995 Stock train approaches Brent Cross station.
Kim Rennie

1995 STOCK (Northern Line)

The 1995 Tube Stock for the Northern Line, replacing 1959 and 1962 Stock trains, was built by GEC Alsthom Metro-Cammell Ltd in Birmingham from sub-assemblies made in Spain, France and Canada. The first train was delivered on 20 December 1996, with further trains arriving over extended periods following commissioning difficulties. Entry into passenger service began on 12 June 1998 and began to replace previous design of stock gradually. The trains are fully equipped for One Person Operation (OPO) and operated in this mode from the outset, guards being replaced in a carefully planned programme. Replacement was completed on 27 January 2000, when the last train of 1959 Stock ran on the Northern Line, ending the employment of guards on the London Underground. By that time 97 out of the 106 new trains had been commissioned for service, which was sufficient for providing the then 84-train peak-hour service. The other nine trains then entered passenger service, the last on 10 April 2001.

The trains share many similarities with the 1996 Stock for the Jubilee Line described below but the body shells of welded aluminium extrusions with honeycomb bracing are slightly more constrained to fit the smaller tunnel gauge. The carriages have longitudinal seating only and in distinction to the 1996 Stock on the Jubilee Line, these Northern Line trains incorporate pairs of tip-up seats by the door stand-backs in the centre section of the saloon. Six LED scrolling visual display units operate under automatic control in each car, along with automated audio station announcements and a driver-operable Public Address system. In the cab all controls, indications and platform CCTV monitors are situated directly in the train operator's line of sight. The Passenger Alarm equipment offers two-way speech with the driver. Other safety and security-related provision includes in-car CCTV video recording equipment, whilst on the outside there are rubber inter-car gap protectors at the car ends, to prevent passengers falling or being pushed in the space between cars.

The AC traction motor control equipment uses IGBT technology (see Appendix) instead of the gate-turn-off thyristors used on the Jubilee Line trains. The trains are equipped with fully blended dynamic regenerative/rheostatic (see Appendix) and electro-pneumatic friction tread brakes with load control and slip/slide protection. There is one brake block per wheel, on all wheels.

1995 Stock car interior. Note that all grab rails and poles are now coloured bright yellow for best visibility and compliance with equality (disability discrimination) legislation.
Capital Transport

	DM	UNDM	T
Length per car	17.77m	17.77m	17.77m
Width	2.63m	2.63m	2.63m
Height	2.88m	2.88m	2.88m
Weight	29.4 tonnes	27.9 tonnes	21.5 tonnes
Per six-car train	157.6 tonnes		
Total seating capacity per train	200, plus 20 perch seats and 48 tip-up seats. There are also 24 wheelchair spaces.		
Total passenger capacity per train	665		

1996 STOCK (Jubilee Line)

To support the Jubilee Line extension project a completely new fleet of 59 trains was constructed, like the Northern Line stock, by GEC Alsthom Metro-Cammell Ltd from sub-assemblies made in Spain, France and Canada. The trains entered service progressively from Christmas Eve 1997 replacing the former 1983 stock on an old-for-new basis until only the new stock was running in July 1998. Classified 1996 Tube Stock, six cars were provided per train in the form of two three-car units. Provision was made for adding a seventh car to each train subsequently, which took place over the 2005/6 Christmas period, when four new trains were supplied to increase the fleet to 63 trains.

Opposite Visually there is little to distinguish the Jubilee Line's 1996 stock from that provided for the Northern Line in 1995 but there are constructional differences. The train were also designed from the outset for automatic operation, with moving block control that allows trains to run closer together, shortening journey times and increasing the potential number of trains per hour. This view is at West Hampstead. *Brian Hardy*

Above In recent years London Underground has upgraded the rolling stock and signalling/control infrastructure of its tube lines progressively. Several schemes are already complete, such as the Central Line (1990s), Waterloo & City Line (2006) and Jubilee Line (2011). Work on the Victoria Line was completed in July 2012 and is in progress on the Northern Line, with completion scheduled for the end 2014. Yet to start are similar schemes for the Piccadilly and Bakerloo Lines, the latter employing the oldest trains to run on the Underground. This 1996 Stock train is seen at Stratford Market depot. *Kim Rennie*

Mechanically the trains are constructed with aluminium extrusions welded together into a tubular profile known as a monocoque structure. This construction technique saves weight by using the object's external skin rather than internal framework for support. The trains have fully blended dynamic regenerative plus rheostatic (see Appendix) and electro-pneumatic friction tread brakes with load control and slip/slide protection. There is one brake block per wheel, on all wheels.

Internally, the trains are similar to the 1995 Stock of the Northern Line but perch seats replace the tip-up seats. There are six automated LED scrolling visual display units in each car, along with automated audio station announcements and a driver-operable public address system. The passenger alarm offers talkback facility to the driver.

Automatic train operation (see Appendix) was envisaged from the outset, although initially trains ran under conventional one person operation, with trip-cock train protection. From 2011 new signalling technology, known as 'moving block', was implemented on the Jubilee Line, using transmission-based train control (TBTC) equipment and onboard vehicle computers. This provides trains with 'movement authority based on their reported location, speed and the distance to the train ahead whilst ensuring a minimum safe braking distance between trains is maintained, The system allows trains to run closer together, shortening journey times and increasing the potential number of trains per hour.

Train formation was originally in the form of two three-car units coupled together, each comprising a Driving Motor car [DM], Trailer car [T] and an Uncoupling Non-Driving Motor car [UNDM] to create DM–T–UNDM+UNDM–T–DM. After the additional trailers were added the train formation became DM–T–UNDM+UNDM–ST–T–DM, ST being the additional 'special trailer'.

	DM	UNDM	T
Length per car	17.77m	17.77m	17.77m
Width	2.63m	2.63m	2.63m
Height	2.88m	2.88m	2.88m
Weight	29.4 tonnes	26.7 tonnes	20.5 tonnes
Per seven-car train	156 tonnes		
Total seating capacity per train	234, plus 24 wheelchair spaces.		
Total standing capacity per train	583		
Total passenger capacity per train	817		

The interior of 1996 Stock differs from 1995 Stock in the design used on the seat moquette and in the use of perch seats in place of the tip-up seats fitted to the 1995 trains. Poles and grab rails are again coloured yellow. *Capital Transport*

2009 STOCK

Constructed at Derby by Bombardier Transportation UK, the 2009 Tube Stock trains have been a key component of London Underground's upgrade of the Victoria Line. A total of 47 trains have been constructed, with delivery taking place between July 2009 and June 2011.

These trains replaced the 1967 Tube Stock that ran previously on the line and as such they offer significant improvements to operator and passengers alike.

In combination with the new signalling infrastructure that is also part of the line upgrade the new trains will achieve improved reliability, an 8 per cent decrease in journey times between stations and a 16 per cent overall decrease in journey times is due in part to the trains' higher top speed of 50mph (80 km/h). The trains employ IGBT-driven (see Appendix) AC asynchronous electric motors from a 630V supply. The train is capable of regenerative braking (see Appendix) at 790V, significantly improving the energy efficiency of the train. Braking is controlled by the latest technology, Knorr Bremse's EP2002 system which employs data bus links along the train to improve brake effectiveness taking into account a wide range of parameters. Another factor leading to shorter headways and faster journey times is the line's new 'Distance-to-go' signalling system that enables automatic train protection and operation (see Appendix) to be implemented.

Tip-up seats are fitted in the extensive wheelchair provision on the 2009 Stock. *Capital Transport*

Passenger convenience is improved in several ways. The trains are the first on London Underground to comply fully with the Rail Vehicle Accessibility Regulations, with full-sized wheelchair spaces, door threshold lighting and colour-contrasting fittings and displays. Wider doors make for faster boarding and alighting of passengers, reducing dwell times in stations, whilst offset-centre door poles assist wheelchair access. The doors themselves are operated electrically rather than by the pneumatic control employed traditionally on London Underground trains. A significant safety benefit is that the doors are fitted with sensors that can also electronically detect objects preventing the doors closing (initially these caused problems on account of being over-sensitive). Other passenger benefits include audio announcements, clearer electronic displays showing real-time service information and CCTV in every car for improved security.

Dimensionally the new trains are larger than those they replaced. In overall length (133m) the trains are 3m longer than the 1967 Stock, making them the longest in use on London's deep tube lines. They are also slightly (40mm) wider than the 1967 Stock, reflecting the Victoria Line's slightly larger loading gauge. On the positive side, this extra width combined with the trains' thinner bodyshell provides slightly more space for passengers. On the other hand the larger size prevents the stock running over other tube lines.

Each train consists of eight cars, of which six are motored, improving both acceleration rates and braking capability. Within the train there are two four-car units, in the configuration DM –T–NDM–UNDM, each coupled back-to-back.

Opposite Although not clearly visible in this interior view, wider doors on 2009 Stock enable faster boarding and alighting of passengers, whilst offset-centre door poles make access less of an obstacle course for wheelchair users. *Kim Rennie*

Length	133m
Width	2.62m
Height	2.88m
Weight	
Driving motor car 'A'	26.8 tonnes
Trailer 'B'	21.6 tonnes
Non-driving motor 'C'	23.8 tonnes
Uncoupling non-driving motor 'D'	25.2 tonnes
Weight per train	194.8 tonnes
Total seating capacity per eight-car train	288 with another 24 tip-up seats and

four RVAR-compliant wheelchair spaces (or an additional 12 tip-up seats).

Total standing capacity per eight-car train	576
Total passenger capacity per eight-car train	864

London Overground's East London Line is an inspired assemblage of the original East London Line, part of the North London Line and former Network South East lines from New Cross Gate to Crystal Palace and West Croydon. Some impressive views can be had from its trains as seen here near Hoxton. *Capital Transport*

OVERGROUND TRAINS

London Overground Rail Operations Ltd

North London Line train at Stratford station, the eastern end of the line.
Capital Transport

London Overground Rail Operations Ltd (LOROL) is the Train Operating Company (TOC) responsible for running the London Overground network, which it does under a Concession Agreement with Transport for London (TfL). Its routes include the North London Line (Stratford to Richmond), the West London Line (Willesden Junction to Clapham Junction), the extended East London Line (Highbury & Islington to West Croydon and Crystal Palace and Clapham Junction), the Euston to Watford local service (DC line) and the Gospel Oak to Barking service (nick-named the GOBLIN line and the only Overground service operated by diesel trains; the other lines are electrified). The East London Line, between Whitechapel and New Cross and New Cross Gate was previously part of London Underground until December 2007, whilst the other lines were taken over from the Silverlink Trains TOC.

When LOROL took over the Silverlink Metro services it inherited a number of time-worn Class 313 dual-system EMUs as well as the Class 150 DMUs used on the GOBLIN line. Because these trains presented an outdated image and were not capable of economic improvement. London Overground invested more than £260 million in commissioning an impressive fleet of new vehicles that were designed specifically to meet the needs of London Overground passengers, bearing little resemblance to their predecessors. Designed with ease of passenger movement, comfort and security in mind, they provide easier, faster access for everyone (including wheelchair users and passengers with bulky pushchairs or luggage), more space in each carriage thanks to wider doors and gangways along with increased capacity to ease overcrowding during the busiest periods of the day. Other features include air conditioning, real-time information, relayed to customers via on-board audio and visual announcements, greater security thanks to walk-through carriages providing clear sightlines for passengers and CCTV.

Some of London Overground's Class 378 trains (those working on the North London, West London Watford DC lines) have dual-system capability. This means they can operate at 25kV AC from overhead wires or 750 V DC from third rail. This view was taken at Hackney Wick. *Kim Rennie*

CLASS 378 CAPITALSTAR TRAINS

The Class 378 Capitalstar trains, constructed in Derby by Bombardier Transportation UK, are a development of the generic Electrostar design family that includes five other classes operated by rail franchises in the UK at speeds of up to 100mph. All Electrostar trains share a flexible, modular design that allows Bombardier to 'maintain the longevity of the Electrostar platform for both suburban and longer distance applications alike'.

Some of the 378/2s that were delivered for the North London Line and West London Line subsequently moved to the East London Line for its extension to Clapham Junction in December 2012. One is seen at Highbury & Islington. *Capital Transport*

A 378/1 at Wandsworth Road on the Clapham Junction section of the extended East London Line. This is one of two stations on the extension, the other being Clapham High Street, now managed by London Overground. *Kim Rennie*

Both Electrostar and Turbostar (see Class 172 on page 56) trains are built to the same basic design, sharing a bodyshell and core structure that is optimised for rapid manufacturing and simple maintenance. This consists of an underframe, which is created by seam-welding a number of aluminium alloy extrusions, upon which body side panels are mounted followed by a single piece roof, again made from extruded sections. The car ends (cabs) are made from glass-reinforced plastic and steel, and are torque-bolted onto the main car bodies. Below-body components are collected in 'rafts', which are bolted into slots on the underframe extrusion. The mainly aluminium alloy body achieves light weight that aids acceleration and energy efficiency.

The London Overground trains were built in several separate batches, each representing a separate sub-class with different traction characteristics. Class 378/0 is the dual-system (see Appendix) three-car train used initially on the North London and West London Lines, of which 24 three-car units were ordered in 2006. The remaining 20 trains in ordered at the same time were four-car units for the extended East London Line; these are classified 378/1, equipped for third-rail DC operation only.

In 2007 TfL placed an additional order for 24 cars to extend the three-car Class 378/0 trains already in production (on completion these trains were reclassified 378/2) plus three additional four-car units for service on the extended East London Line. A further seven four-car units were ordered in 2008 and another three in 2009, bringing the total number of Capitalstars to 57.

Summarising, Capitalstar trains are split into two types: 20 four-car DC-only ELL trains (378/1) and 37 dual-system four-car trains (378/2). The 378/2s were initially all allocated to the NLL and WLL but some have since been transferred to the ELL for its extension to Clapham Junction.

All Capitalstar trains feature:
- High passenger capacity, described as commuter-friendly, achieved by providing 100% longitudinal seating and wide centre aisles for standing passengers
- Better security with driver-monitored onboard CCTV and clear sight-lines for passengers
- Wider aisles for quicker boarding and alighting
- Better journey ambience, with wider seats, more handrails and air conditioning (the windows are capable of being unlocked in an emergency)
- Improved accessibility, with dedicated wheelchair bays
- Real time information, with audio and visual announcements.

Longitudinal seating and wide centre aisles make for high passenger capacity and a major improvement in appearance over the trains that preceded them. The faded looking seat far right is in fact covered in a variation of the moquette colouring to indicate a priority seat for those less able to stand.
Capital Transport

Two pairs of double doors are provided on either side of each car, described as sliding pocket doors (these open and close more quickly than plug doors). Wide gangway connections are provided between cars within each train set, also an emergency exit at the centre of each outer end of the train.

Unlike London Underground stock that operates partly over Network Rail lines the outer ends of these units are painted in warning yellow.

Length	20.4m
Width	2.80m
Height	3.78m
Weight	159.5 tonnes
Seating	36 (driving motor cars), 34 (trailer car)
Total seating capacity per four-car train	140 plus 12 'perches'
Total standing capacity per four-car train	354
Total passenger capacity per four-car train	494

CLASS 172 TURBOSTAR TRAINS

London Overground operates eight two-car Class 172s on the Gospel Oak to Barking Line, replacing the previous operator's Class 150 stock. These are by necessity diesel trains, as the line is not electrified and a cost-benefit case for electrification has not been identified. The trains entered service in 2010 and belong to the Turbostar family of diesel multiple units (DMUs) made by Bombardier Transportation UK of Derby. This particular variant of the family is known as 172/0; other types include three-car sets and trains fitted with corridor connections at each end.

The manufacturer described the Class 172 as the 'greenest' train it has ever made. Weighing less than previous classes of DMU, the train's fuel consumption and carbon dioxide reductions are both reduced. More than 90 per cent of its construction materials are recyclable.

'Turbostar' 172005 is seen at Richmond on 26 November 2010 after having worked part of the evening peak shuttle (Richmond-Willesden-Richmond) due to two Class 378s failing and another having been sent to Derby for 4-car conversion. The 172s are normally confined to the diesels-only Goblin Line between Gospel Oak to Barking. *Julian Gajewski*

Seating capacity is 120 seats, which is a smaller number than the Class 150 trains that they replaced. To compensate for this increased room is provided for standing passengers together with wider aisles in the doorways to reduce dwell time at stations for boarding and alighting. Two sets of passenger doors are provided on either side per car, of the double-leaf sliding plug type. No opening windows are provided, as the trains are provided with air conditioning. One car out of every pair has a toilet, whilst public address, CCTV and a Passenger Information System are provided.

In 2012 TfL invited tenders for the provision of eight three or four-car diesel trains to replace the Class 172 units, which are unable to handle peak passenger loads.

Length	23.62m	**Weight**	43.1 tonnes
Width	2.69m	**Total seating capacity for two cars**	120
Height	3.77m		

AFTERLIFE

Some former London Underground stock remains in service elsewhere. There are also a number of examples on various preserved railways and a few in private ownership. The London Transport Museum is another place to see old Underground cars.

A train of 1938 Tube Stock prepares to head north from the southern terminus of the Island Line at Shanklin. *Brian Hardy*

Island Line train interior with modernised lighting. *Brian Hardy*

Isle of Wight

An older design of London Underground train, known as the 1938 Stock, is in use on the Island Line rail franchise on the Isle of Wight. This line runs from Ryde Pier Head southwards for 8½ miles (13.7 km) to Shanklin and was electrified at 630V DC on the third-rail system in 1967, when the remainder of the island's rail system was closed. The low ceiling of Ryde Tunnel means that rolling stock of standard height cannot be used on the line and initially ex-London Transport Standard Stock (built between 1923 and 1934) was used, being replaced progressively from July 1989 until 1992 by the 1938 Stock currently in use.

The five two-car multiple unit trains in use are termed Class 483 and were refurbished between 1989 and 1992.

Further reading: Hardy, Brian (2003). *Tube Trains on the Isle of Wight*. London: Capital Transport. ISBN 1-85414-276-3.

Alderney (Channel Islands)

The Alderney Railway, which opened in 1847, is one of the oldest and least known railway lines in the British Isles. It was constructed by the British government to convey stone from the eastern end of the Island to build the breakwater and the Victorian forts. Since 1980 passenger services have been run by the Alderney Railway Society, currently using a diesel locomotive hauling two 1959 tube cars from London Underground (numbered 1044 and 1045) that were acquired in 2001 to replace two 1938 Stock cars that had succumbed to the salty sea air.

Further details of the railway and its timetables are given in its website, http://www.alderneyrailway.com.

Above A recreation of a Metropolitan Railway train at Sheffield Park station on the Bluebell Railway in Sussex. The locomotive, E class 0-4-4T No. 1, was built in 1898 and is normally stabled at the Buckinghamshire Railway Centre at Quainton Road. It visited the Bluebell Line in July 2007 to celebrate the restoration of that railway's four Metropolitan Railway coaches built between 1898 and 1900. Loco No.1 was restored during 2012 for London Underground's 150th anniversary celebrations in 2013. *Brian Hardy*

Left Considerable effort went into the restoration of these vintage carriages, with new varnished teak panels replacing previous patching up with plywood and steel. The seats were retrimmed in a reproduction moquette fabric of the London Transport era, produced by the original manufacturer using the original loom cards, with collaboration by the London Transport Museum. *Brian Hardy*

The Spa Valley Railway at Tunbridge Wells has two of these former Metropolitan T Stock motor cars, which spent their last years of life with the Underground as Sleet Locomotives in the engineers' fleet. *Brian Hardy*

The Mangapps Farm Railway at Burnham on Crouch, Essex, owns three Underground cars – R Stock motor car 22624, 1959 Tube Stock motor car 1030 in Heritage livery (just visible in this view of 22624) and 1959 trailer car 2044. It also has Permaquip track maintenance machine 94801 from the Waterloo & City Line. *Brian Hardy*

ENGINEERS' TRAINS

1965-built Metro-Cammell battery loco L24 has been rebuilt in Acton Works as a prototype refurbishment. The most obvious changes are larger driver's cabs, which mean that access is now via walkways above the buffer beams, and high-intensity headlights. In this view, the modified loco leads at Turnham Green on a test train working. Other battery locomotives are in the process of being similarly modified.
Kim Rennie

The vehicles of London Underground's service stock fleet are maintained by 'TransPlant' which embraces the operation of the network's engineers' trains. The mainstay of London Underground's service stock locomotives are 29 battery locomotives built between 1964 and 1974, comprising 18 Metro-Cammell locomotives (L20-32 built in 1964 and L15-19 built in 1970-71). The other 11 locomotives (L44-54) were built by BREL at Doncaster in 1973-74, which allowed some older machines to be withdrawn. Six locomotives (L62-L67) that were built in 1985 but were non-standard were withdrawn after a few years' service and were finally scrapped in 2012. Also recently scrapped is the Tunnel Cleaning Train of 1976/77 vintage and the two Weed Killing Ballast Motor Cars converted from 1938 Tube Stock in 1978.

Apart from the erstwhile L62-67, all of the battery locomotives described above had hinged buffers which were swung back when coupling to vehicles of tube stock height – the design was basically unchanged (apart from minor variations) from that first used in 1938. All locomotives have a cab at each end and are built to tube loading gauge. They are able to operate direct from current, or by battery power and are most often used to operate engineers' trains, mainly at night during non-traffic hours. Various modifications have been made to the battery locomotives in recent years, most noticeably the fitting of high-intensity headlights, replacement of the swing-back buffers by spring buffers, and the fitting of buckeye couplers. More recently, work began to modify the remaining locomotives with a revised front end and improved battery access. The locomotives modified so far are identified as such in the table.

Two Pilot Motor cars, converted from 1960 Tube Stock driving motor cars 3901 and 3905, are for working with the Track Recording car (which was converted by BREL at Derby from 1973 stock trailer 514 in 1987). This three-car train is likely to be withdrawn and replaced by a six-car 'Asset Inspection Train', which is currently under conversion and testing. It comprises a four-car unit of 1972 MkI Tube Stock and (in the middle) two 1967 Tube Stock driving motor cars. Entry into service for the new train is expected in 2013 although the Track Recording Train may survive a little longer.

A new Tunnel Cleaning Train is under construction and will comprise seven vehicles. Motive power will be provided by two pairs of 1967 Tube Stock DMs, in between which will be three purpose-built cars. The equipment is being supplied by Hanover-based metro cleaning vehicles specialist Schörling Kommunal. A hydraulic drive will allow low-speed running at 1 km/h during cleaning, while the motor cars will enable the train to reach work sites at normal line speed.

For the construction and equipping of the Jubilee Line Extension, 14 diesel locomotives were built by Schöma of Germany to haul a dedicated fleet of 15 general purpose wagons, four bogie well wagons and four 4-wheel cable drum wagons, all built by Bombardier. The 32-tonne diesel locomotives were built to tube loading gauge suitable for working in tube tunnels. They are fitted with normal-height buffers and drop-head buckeye couplers. Once construction of the JLE was complete, the locomotives and wagons passed into the Transplant fleet in 1999.

The fleet of miscellaneous vehicles has changed very little since the final edition of *London Underground Rolling Stock* was published in 2002, apart from the scrapping of a handful of vehicles and some others modified for use with the changing demands of the type of work undertaken. A new points and crossings tamping machine (TMM774) built by Franz-Plasser of Linz, Austria, was delivered in 2007.

Mobile diesel crane C623. Four of these are in use, numbered C623 to C626. *Kim Rennie*

Plasser & Theurer ballast tamping machine TMM773 'Alan Jenkins' (this is probably an unofficial naming in honour of the tube worker, union activist and whistle-blower of this name). The fleet contains four machines of this type, numbered 771, 772, 773 and 774. The first three can pass through deep-level tubes but 774 can work on sub-surface lines only. *Kim Rennie*

Plasser & Theurer ballast tamping machine 774. This machine cannot work through deep-level tubes. The purpose of these machines is to pack or compress track ballast, a process known as tamping. This is necessary because train movement over ballasted track tends to cause the ballast to shift and settle, leading to uneven support for the track and a bumpy ride for passengers. *Kim Rennie*

Diesel Locomotive No. 6, 'Denise', built by Schoma, Germany in 1996. Supplied originally for work on the Jubilee Line Extension, these locomotives have exceptionally low emissions, enabling them to work in tube tunnels. *Kim Rennie*

Battery loco L48 of 1973 and companion at Hammersmith (Hammersmith & City Line) station. Behind the train is what is left of a remarkable painted advertisement, dating from the 1930s, for the Hammersmith Palace ballroom and entertainment venue. This operated until 2007 and although the structure itself was demolished in 2012, the wall remains. *Kim Rennie*

Four Schoma diesel locos together, from left to right nos. 8 'Emma', 10 'Clementine', 9 'Debora' and 4 'Pam'. All are named after secretaries of works managers on the Jubilee Line Extension project. The location is Lillie Bridge depot. *Kim Rennie*

This three-car train is used for track recording purposes, i.e. regular checks of the track geometry. The track recording car is a former 1973 Stock trailer and this is coupled between two Cravens built 1960 Stock motor cars to travel around the system. The 1960 Tube Stock was intended as a new fleet of trains for the Central Line but did not get beyond the prototype stage. *Mark Kehoe*

Known as the Asset Inspection Train (AIT) or Unit 3213, this provides the permanent way engineer with a technical assessment of the state of the track. This four-car train of 1972 (Mk 1) tube stock was withdrawn from passenger service on 2 November 1998 and after overhaul in 2006 converted for its present role at Doncaster. Two cars of 1967 stock were added in the middle of the formation in November 2011, as shown here. *Kim Rennie*

Car 6036 is part of the Rail Adhesion Train, made up of A Stock and used in London Underground's autumn battle against 'leaves on the line'. Compressed leaves on the rail head form a hard, slippery coating that in damp conditions leads to low adhesion and the risk of extended braking distances and hence station and signal overruns. Particular problems exist with leaf fall beyond Harrow-on-the-Hill and Leytonstone. The solution is to apply a sand/gel mix called Sandite from a special train to mitigate the contamination. *Kim Rennie*

ENGINEERS' VEHICLE LIST

Unless noted otherwise, locomotives are in yellow livery.

Diesel Locomotives 14

Built 1996 by Schoma, Germany. All fitted with Jubilee/Northern Line TBTC signalling system.

No.	Name	No.	Name
1 *	Britta Lotta	8	Emma
2 †	Nikki	9	Debora
3 †	Claire	10	Clementine
4	Pam	11	Joan
5 *	Sophie	12	Melanie
6	Denise	13	Michele
7	Annemarie	14	Carol

*   Fitted with tube stock height wedgelock coupler.
†   Fitted with emergency coupler as on battery locomotives.

Battery Locomotives 29

	No.	Deliv.	Builder		No.	Deliv.	Builder
‡	L15	1970	Metro-Cammell		L30	1965	Metro-Cammell
‡	L16	1970	Metro-Cammell	*	L31	1965	Metro-Cammell
‡	L17	1971	Metro-Cammell		L32	1965	Metro-Cammell
‡	L18	1971	Metro-Cammell	†‡	L44	1974	BREL Doncaster
‡	L19	1971	Metro-Cammell	‡	L45	1974	BREL Doncaster
‡	L20	1964	Metro-Cammell	†‡	L46	1974	BREL Doncaster
‡	L21	1964	Metro-Cammell	‡	L47	1974	BREL Doncaster
	L22	1965	Metro-Cammell	†‡	L48	1974	BREL Doncaster
	L23	1965	Metro-Cammell	†‡	L49	1974	BREL Doncaster
*	L24	1965	Metro-Cammell	†‡	L50	1974	BREL Doncaster
*	L25	1965	Metro-Cammell	†‡	L51	1974	BREL Doncaster
*	L26	1965	Metro-Cammell	†‡	L52	1974	BREL Doncaster
*	L27	1965	Metro-Cammell	†‡	L53	1974	BREL Doncaster
	L28	1965	Metro-Cammell	†‡	L54	1974	BREL Doncaster
	L29	1965	Metro-Cammell				

All locomotives are fitted with emergency couplers.
†   Painted blue.
*   Modified cab ends. (All locomotives to be modified with L23 and L30 work in progress).
‡   Fitted with Central Line ATP and Jubilee/Northern Line TBTC signalling.

Bogie Flat Wagons (30 tons capacity) 3

No.	Built by
F351	1951 Gloucester
F355	1951 Gloucester
F398	1965 BR Ashford

F351 and F355 operate as a permanently-coupled pair.

Bogie Hopper Wagons (30 tonnes capacity) 22
Built by W.H. Davis 1981

HW201	HW204	HW207	HW210	HW213	HW216	HW219	HW222
HW202	HW205	HW208	HW211	HW214	HW217	HW220	
HW203	HW206	HW209	HW212	HW215	HW218	HW221	

First Generation Rail Wagons (20 tons capacity) 8

No.	Built	No.	Built	No.	Built
RW491	1958 Gloucester	RW494 †	1958 Gloucester	RW505	1965 BR Ashford
RW492	1958 Gloucester	RW495 ‡	1965 BR Ashford	RW506	1965 BR Ashford
RW493	1958 Gloucester	RW499 †	1965 BR Ashford		

†   Restricted to Ruislip depot use only.
‡   Fitted with chute for operating with long welded rail train.

Diesel Cranes 6

No.	Builder	Year	No.	Builder	Year
C623 *	Cowan Sheldon	1982	DHC627 †	Cowan Sheldon	1986
C624 *	Cowan Sheldon	1984	DHC628 †	Cowan Boyd	1993
C625 *	Cowan Sheldon	1984			
C626 *	Cowan Sheldon	1984			

*   7½-tonne crane
†   10-tonne twin-jib crane

Plasser Track Maintenance Machines 4

No.	Date New	Type
TMM771 *	1980	PU0716 Plasser-Theurer Tamping Machine
TMM772	1980	PU0716 Plasser-Theurer Tamping Machine
TMM773 *†	1980	PU0716 Plasser-Theurer Tamping Machine
TMM774	2007	08-275-4ZW Points and crossings tamping Machine built by Franz-Plasser of Linz, Austria

*   Fitted with Jubilee/Northern Line TBTC signalling.
†   Named 'Alan Jenkins'.

Unimog Road/Rail Vehicles 2

No.	Date	Reg. No.
L84	1983	A456NWX
L85	1986	C622EWT

Rail Wagons (20 tonnes capacity) 26
Built 1986 by Procor, fitted with buckeye couplers

RW801 †	RW805 ‡	RW809	RW812	RW815 §	RW818 ‡	RW821 ‡	RW824 *
RW802 †	RW806 ‡	RW810	RW813	RW816 §	RW819 ‡	RW822 *	RW825 *
RW803 †	RW807	RW811	RW814 #	RW817 §	RW820 §	RW823 *	RW826 *
RW804 †	RW808						

*   Long welded rail train. RW822 and RW826 fitted with chute.
†   Fitted with side-operated electric cranes (trade name 'ELK' equipment).
‡   Fitted with End Loading Unit for loading rail over the headstock.
§   Fitted with de-icing equipment. (To be removed from RW817 and to be fitted to another wagon).
#   Currently being converted to tunnel ring replacement wagon.

High-Deck Wagons (40 tonnes capacity) 6
Built 1987 by Procor, fitted with buckeye couplers

HD871 *   HD872   HD873   HD874   HD875 *   HD876

* Fitted with hand-operated winch units.

General Purpose Wagons (30 tonnes capacity) 41
Built 1985 by Procor

GP901 ‡	GP907	GP912	GP917	GP922	GP927	GP932	GP937
GP902	GP908 *	GP913	GP918	GP923	GP928	GP933 †	GP938
GP903	GP909	GP914	GP919	GP924	GP929 †	GP934	GP939
GP904	GP910	GP915	GP920	GP925 †	GP930	GP935	GP940
GP905	GP911	GP916	GP921	GP926 †	GP931	GP936	GP941
GP906							

*   Fitted with equipment for weedkilling. Operates between battery locomotives.
†   Fitted with cable turntables.
‡   Fitted with Roll Loader Crane.

Former Cement Mixer/Match Wagons 12
Built 1987 by Procor, fitted with buckeye couplers.

CM950	CM952	CM954	MW956	MW958	MW960
CM951	CM953	CM955	MW957	MW959	MW961

Four wagons form two 'Tubevac' (ballast sucker) trains in the formation CM951-CM955 and CM954-MW958. Each pair operates with a general purpose wagon (JLE1 and JLE2). CM 951 and CM954 contain the diesel units, while CM955 and MW958 contain the ballast sucking equipment. MW959-MW960 and MW956-MW961 operate as pairs.

Cable Well Wagons 3
CW1053   CW1054   CW1055   Built 1996 by Bombardier

General Purpose Wagons ex-Jubilee Line Extension 15
Built 1994 by Bombardier

JLE1 *	JLE3 *	JLE5	JLE7	JLE9	JLE11	JLE13	JLE15
JLE2 *	JLE4	JLE6	JLE8	JLE10	JLE12	JLE14	

*   Fitted with Palfinger crane to operate with CM954-MW958 (JLE2) and CM951-CM955 (JLE1).

Bogie Well Wagons ex-Jubilee Line Extension 4
Built 1994 by Bombardier

JLE16 *   JLE17   JLE18   JLE19

*   Fitted with de-icing equipment.

4-wheel Cable Drum Wagons ex-Jubilee Line Extension 4
Built 1994 by Bombardier

JLE20   JLE21   JLE22   JLE23

Turbot Wagons (34 tonnes capacity) 60

Built 1982-1988 variously by BR Shildon and Swindon, and RFS Doncaster. Converted by ABB Crewe in 1995. SB231-239 have 'long' drawgear, SB 240-290 'short' drawgear.

	No.	Former DB No.		No.	Former DB No.		No.	Former DB No.
SB	231	978865	SB	251	978753	SB	271	978617
SB	232	978047	SB	252	978884	SB	272	978669
SB	233	978916	SB	253	978767	SB	273	978678
SB	234	978864	SB	254	978143	SB	274	978682
SB	235	978820	SB	255	978886	SB	275	978685
SB	236	978702	SB	256	978653	SB	276	978688
SB	237	978677	SB	257	978626	SB	277	978773
SB	238	987788	SB	258	978016	SB	278	978783
SB	239	978809	SB	259	978026	SB	279	978787
SB	240	978647	SB	260	978028	SB	280	978797
SB	241	978652	SB	261	978051	SB	281	978808
SB	242	978766	SB	262	978076	SB	282	978810
SB	243	978897	SB	263	978086	SB	283	978824
SB	244	978898	SB	264	978145	SB	284	978830
SB	245	978088	SB	265	978161	SB	285	978846
SB	246	978901	SB	266	978211	SB	286	978858
SB	247	978628	SB	267	978318	SB	287	978869
SB	248	978003	SB	268	978408	SB	288	978892
SB	249	978614	SB	269	978420	SB	289	978895
SB	250	978700	SB	270	978608	SB	290	978918

Track Recording Train 1

No.	Date	Converted	Orig. No.	Built	Type
L132	1960	1987 BREL	3901	Cravens	Pilot Motor
TRC666	1973	1987 BREL	514	Metro-Cammell	Track Recording car
L133	1960	1987 BREL	3905	Cravens	Pilot Motor

L132 and L133 are fitted with buckeye couplers at inner ends at 'main line' height. Fitted with Central Line ATP only. TRC666 is fitted with buckeye couplers at 'main line' height.

The Track Recording Train is to be replaced by a six-car 'Asset Inspection Train', which has been converted from 1967 and 1972 MkI Tube Stock. Its formation is 3213-4213-3179+3079-4313-3313 and is currently being modified before entering service.

BAKERLOO LINE 1972 MKII TUBE STOCK

4-CAR 'A'-END UNITS				3-CAR 'D' END UNITS		
DM SOUTH LEADING	TRAILER	TRAILER	DM NORTH MIDDLE	UNDM SOUTH MIDDLE	TRAILER	DM NORTH LEADING
3231	4231	4331	3331	3431	4531	3531
3232	4232	4332	3332	3432	4532	3532
3233	4233	4333	3333	3433	4533	3533
3234	4234	4334	3334	3434	4534	3534
3235	4235	4335	3335	3435	4535	3535
3236	4236	4336	3336	3436	4536	3536
3237	4237	4337	3337	3437	4537	3537
3238	4238	4338	3338	3438	4538	3538
3239	4239	4339	3339	3440	4540	3540
3240	4240	4340	3340	3441	4541	3541
3241	4241	4341	3341	3442	4542	3542
3242	4242	4342	3342	3443	4543	3543
3243	4243	4343	3343	3444	4544	3544
3244	4244	4344	3344	3445	4545	3545
3245	4245	4345	3345	3446	4546	3546
3246	4246	4346	3346	3447	4547	3547
3247	4247	4347	3347	3448	4548	3548
3248	4248	4348	3348	3449	4549	3549
3250	4250	4350	3350	3450	4550	3550
3251	4251	4351	3351	3451	4551	3551
3252	4252	4352(D)	3352	3452	4552	3552
3253	4253	4353(D)	3353	3453	4553	3553
3254	4254	4354(D)	3354	3454	4554	3554
3255	4255	4355(D)	3355	3455	4555	3555
3256	4256	4356(D)	3356	3456	4556	3556
3258	4258	4358(D)	3358	3457	4557	3557
3259	4259	4359(D)	3359	3458	4558	3558
3260	4260	4360(D)	3360	3459	4559	3559
3261	4261	4361(D)	3361	3460	4560	3560
3262	4262	4362(D)	3362	3461	4561	3561
3263	4263	4363(D)	3363	3462	4562	3562
3264*	4264*	4364*	3364*	3463	4563	3563
3265*	4265*	4365*	3365^	3464*	4564*	3564*
3266*	4266*	4366†	3366†	3465*	4565*	3565*
3267*	4267*	4367*	3367*	3466*	4566*	3566*
				3467*	4567*	3567*

DM SOUTH LEADING	TRAILER	TRAILER	UNDM NORTH MIDDLE
3299†	4299†	4399†	3399†

(D) Fitted with de-icing equipment.
* 1972 MkI Stock cars renumbered.
† 1972 MkII Stock cars renumbered.

UNIT FORMATIONS

Passenger stock on London Underground and London Overground is formed into semi-permanent unit formations to make up trains of three, four, five, six, seven or eight cars. On the following pages the units that form each train for each line are listed

CENTRAL LINE 1992 TUBE STOCK TWO-CAR 'A' - 'B' UNITS

DM 'A' CAR	NDM 'B' CAR	DM 'A' CAR	NDM 'B' CAR	DM 'A' CAR	NDM 'B' CAR	DM 'A' CAR	NDM 'B' CAR
91001	92001	91089	92089	91177	92177	91265	92265
91003	92003	91091	92091	91179	92179	91267	92267
91005	92005	91093	92093	91181	92181	91269	92269
91007	92007	91095	92095	91183	92183	91271	92271
91009	92009	91097	92097	91185	92185	91273	92273
91011	92011	91099	92099	91187	92187	91275	92275
91013	92013	91101	92101	91189	92189	91277	92277
91015	92015	91103	92103	91191	92191	91279	92279
91017	92017	91105	92105	91193	92193	91281	92281
91019	92019	91107	92107	91195	92195	91283	92283
91021	92021	91109	92109	91197	92197	91285	92285
91023	92023	91111	92111	91199	92199	91287	92287
91025	92025	91113	92113	91201	92201	91289	92289
91027	92027	91115	92115	91203	92203	91291	92291
91029	92029	91117	92117	91205	92205	91293	92293
91031	92031	91119	92119	91207	92207	91295	92295
91033	92033	91121	92121	91209	92209	91297	92297
91035	92035	91123	92123	91211	92211	91299	92299
91037	92037	91125	92125	91213	92213	91301	92301
91039	92039	91127	92127	91215	92215	91303	92303
91041	92041	91129	92129	91217	92217	91305	92305
91043	92043	91131	92131	91219	92219	91307	92307
91045	92045	91133	92133	91221	92221	91309	92309
91047	92047	91135	92135	91223	92223	91311	92311
91049	92049	91137	92137	91225	92225	91313	92313
91051	92051	91139	92139	91227	92227	91315	92315
91053	92053	91141	92141	91229	92229	91317	92317
91055	92055	91143	92143	91231	92231	91319	92319
91057	92057	91145	92145	91233	92233	91321	92321
91059	92059	91147	92147	91235	92235	91323	92323
91061	92061	91149	92149	91237	92237	91325	92325
91063	92063	91151	92151	91239	92239	91327	92327
91065	92065	91153	92153	91241	92241	91329	92329
91067	92067	91155	92155	91243	92243	91331	92331
91069	92069	91157	92157	91245	92245	91333	92333
91071	92071	91159	92159	91247	92247	91335	92335
91073	92073	91161	92161	91249	92249	91337	92337
91075	92075	91163	92163	91251	92251	91339	92339
91077	92077	91165	92165	91253	92253	91341	92341
91079	92079	91167	92167	91255	92255	91343	92343
91081	92081	91169	92169	91257	92257	91345	92345
91083	92083	91171	92171	91259	92259	91347	92347
91085	92085	91173	92173	91261	92261	91349	92349
91087	92087	91175	92175	91263	92263		

1992 TUBE STOCK TWO-CAR 'B' - 'C' UNITS

NDM 'B' CAR	NDM 'C' CAR	NDM 'B' CAR	NDM 'C' CAR	NDM 'B' CAR	NDM 'C' CAR	NDM 'B' CAR	NDM 'C' CAR
92002	93002	92070	93070	92138	93138	92206	93206
92004	93004	92072	93072	92140	93140	92208	93208
92006	93006	92074	93074	92142	93142	92210	93210
92008	93008	92076	93076	92144	93144	92212	93212
92010	93010	92078	93078	92146	93146	92214	93214
92012	93012	92080	93080	92148	93148	92216	93216
92014	93014	92082	93082	92150	93150	92218	93218
92016	93016	92084	93084	92152	93152	92220	93220
92018	93018	92086	93086	92154	93154	92222	93222
92020	93020	92088	93088	92156	93156	92224	93224
92022	93022	92090	93090	92158	93158	92226	93226
92024	93024	92092	93092	92160	93160	92228	93228
92026	93026	92094	93094	92162	93162	92230	93230
92028	93028	92096	93096	92164	93164	92232	93232
92030	93030	92098	93098	92166	93166	92234	93234
92032	93032	92100	93100	92168	93168	92236	93236
92034	93034	92102	93102	92170	93170	92238	93238
92036	93036	92104	93104	92172	93172	92240	93240
92038	93038	92106	93106	92174	93174	92242	93242
92040	93040	92108	93108	92176	93176	92244	93244
92042	93042	92110	93110	92178	93178	92246	93246
92044	93044	92112	93112	92180	93180	92248	93248
92046	93046	92114	93114	92182	93182	92250	93250
92048	93048	92116	93116	92184	93184	92252	93252
92050	93050	92118	93118	92186	93186	92254	93254
92052	93052	92120	93120	92188	93188	92256	93256
92054	93054	92122	93122	92190	93190	92258	93258
92056	93056	92124	93124	92192	93192	92260	93260
92058	93058	92126	93126	92194	93194	92262	93262
92060	93060	92128	93128	92196	93196	92264	93264
92062	93062	92130	93130	92198	93198	92266	93266
92064	93064	92132	93132	92200	93200		
92066	93066	92134	93134	92202	93202		
92068	93068	92136	93136	92204	93204		

1992 TUBE STOCK TWO-CAR 'B' - 'D' DE-ICING UNITS

NDM 'B' CAR	NDM 'D' CAR	NDM 'B' CAR	NDM 'D' CAR	NDM 'B' CAR	NDM 'D' CAR	NDM 'B' CAR	NDM 'D' CAR
92402	93402	92418	93418	92434	93434	92450	93450
92404	93404	92420	93420	92436	93436	92452	93452
92406	93406	92422	93422	92438	93438	92454	93454
92408	93408	92424	93424	92440	93440	92456	93456
92410	93410	92426	93426	92442	93442	92458	93458
92412	93412	92428	93428	92444	93444	92460	93460
92414	93414	92430	93430	92446	93446	92462	93462
92416	93416	92432	93432	92448	93448	92464	93464

DM (A)	M1	M2	MS	MS	M1	DM (D)
21302	22302	25302(D)	24302	24301	22301	21301
21304	22304	25304(D)	24304	24303	22303	21303
21306	22306	25306(D)	24306	24305	22305	21305
21308	22308	25308(D)	24308	24307	22307	21307
21310	22310	25310(D)	24310	24309	22309	21309
21312	22312	25312(D)	24312	24311	22311	21311
21314	22314	25314(D)	24314	24313	22313	21313
21316	22316	25316(D)	24316	24315	22315	21315
21318	22318	25318(D)	24318	24317	22317	21317
21320*	22320	25320(D)	24320	24319	22319	21319
21322	22322	25322(D)	24322	24321	22321	21321
21324*	22324	25324(D)	24324	24323	22323	21323
21326	22326	25326(D)	24326	24325	22325	21325
21328*	22328	25328(D)	24328	24327	22327	21327
21330	22330	25330(D)	24330	24329	22329	21329
21332	22332	25332(D)	24332	24331	22331	21331
21334	22334	25334(D)	24334	24333	22333	21333
21336	22336	25336(D)	24336	24335	22335	21335
21338	22338	25338(D)	24338	24337	22337	21337
21340	22340	25340(D)	24340	24339	22339	21339
21342	22342	25342(D)	24342	24341	22341	21341
21344	22344	25344(D)	24344	24343	22343	21343
21346	22346	25346(D)	24346	24345	22345	21345
21348	22348	25348(D)	24348	24347	22347	21347
21350	22350	25350(D)	24350	24349	22349	21349
21352	22352	25352(D)	24352	24351	22351	21351
21354	22354	25354(D)	24354	24353	22353	21353
21356	22356	25356(D)	24356	24355	22355	21355
21358	22358	25358(D)	24358	24357	22357	21357
21360	22360	25360(D)	24360	24359	22359	21359
21362	22362	25362(D)	24362	24361	22361	21361
21364	22364	25364(D)	24364	24363	22363	21363
21366	22366	25366(D)	24366	24365	22365	21365
21368	22368	25368(D)	24368	24367	22367	21367
21370	22370	25370(D)	24370	24369	22369	21369
21372	22372	25372(D)	24372	24371	22371	21371
21374	22374	25374(D)	24374	24373	22373	21373
21376	22376	25376(D)	24376	24375	22375	21375
21378	22378	25378(D)	24378	24377	22377	21377
21380	22380	25380(D)	24380	24379	22379	21379
21382	22382	25382(D)	24382	24381	22381	21381
21384	22384	25384(D)	24384	24383	22383	21383
21386	22386	25386(D)	24386	24385	22385	21385
21388	22388	23388	24388	24387	22387	21387
21390	22390	23390	24390	24389	22389	21389
21392	22392	23392	24392	24391	22391	21391
21394	22394	23394	24394	24393	22393	21393
21396	22396	23396	24396	24395	22395	21395
21398	22398	23398	24398	24397	22397	21397
21400	22400	23400	24400	24399	22399	21399
21402	22402	23402	24402	24401	22401	21401
21404	22404	23404	24404	24403	22403	21403
21406	22406	23406	24406	24405	22405	21405
21408	22408	23408	24408	24407	22407	21407
21410	22410	23410	24410	24409	22409	21409
21412	22412	23412	24412	24411	22411	21411
21414	22414	23414	24414	24413	22413	21413
21416	22416	23416	24416	24415	22415	21415
21418	22418	23418	24418	24417	22417	21417
21420	22420	23420	24420	24419	22419	21419
21422	22422	23422	24422	24421	22421	21421
21424	22424	23424	24424	24423	22423	21423
21426	22426	23426	24426	24425	22425	21425
21428	22428	23428	24428	24427	22427	21427
21430	22430	23430	24430	24429	22429	21429
21432	22432	23432	24432	24431	22431	21431
21434	22434	23434	24434	24433	22433	21433
21436	22436	23436	24436	24435	22435	21435
21438	22438	23438	24438	24437	22437	21437

DM (A)	M1	M2	MS	MS	M1	DM (D)
21440	22440	23440	24440	24439	22439	21439
21442	22442	23442	24442	24441	22441	21441
21444	22444	23444	24444	24443	22443	21443
21446	22446	23446	24446	24445	22445	21445
21448	22448	23448	24448	24447	22447	21447
21450	22450	23450	24450	24449	22449	21449
21452	22452	23452	24452	24451	22451	21451
21454	22454	23454	24454	24453	22453	21453
21456	22456	23456	24456	24455	22455	21455
21458	22458	23458	24458	24457	22457	21457
21460	22460	23460	24460	24459	22459	21459
21462	22462	23462	24462	24461	22461	21461
21464	22464	23464	24464	24463	22463	21463
21466	22466	23466	24466	24465	22465	21465
21468	22468	23468	24468	24467	22467	21467
21470	22470	23470	24470	24469	22469	21469
21472	22472	23472	24472	24471	22471	21471
21474	22474	23474	24474	24473	22473	21473
21476	22476	23476	24476	24475	22475	21475
21478	22478	23478	24478	24477	22477	21477
21480	22480	23480	24480	24479	22479	21479
21482	22482	23482	24482	24481	22481	21481
21484	22484	23484	24484	24483	22483	21483
21486	22486	23486	24486	24485	22485	21485
21488	22488	23488	24488	24487	22487	21487
21490	22490	23490	24490	24489	22489	21489
21492	22492	23492	24492	24491	22491	21491
21494	22494	23494	24494	24493	22493	21493
21496	22496	23496	24496	24495	22495	21495
21498	22498	23498	24498	24497	22497	21497
21500	22500	23500	24500	24499	22499	21499
21502	22502	23502	24502	24501	22501	21501
21504	22504	23504	24504	24503	22503	21503
21506	22506	23506	24506	24505	22505	21505
21508	22508	23508	24508	24507	22507	21507
21510	22510	23510	24510	24509	22509	21509
21512	22512	23512	24512	24511	22511	21511
21514	22514	23514	24514	24513	22513	21513
21516	22516	23516	24516	24515	22515	21515
21518	22518	23518	24518	24517	22517	21517
21520	22520	23520	24520	24519	22519	21519
21522	22522	23522	24522	24521	22521	21521
21524	22524	23524	24524	24523	22523	21523
21526	22526	23526	24526	24525	22525	21525
21528	22528	23528	24528	24527	22527	21527
21530	22530	23530	24530	24529	22529	21529
21532	22532	23532	24532	24531	22531	21531
21534	22534	23534	24534	24533	22533	21533
21536	22536	23536	24536	24535	22535	21535
21538	22538	23538	24538	24537	22537	21537
21540	22540	23540	24540	24539	22539	21539
21542	22542	23542	24542	24541	22541	21541
21544	22544	23544	24544	24543	22543	21543
21546	22546	23546	24546	24545	22545	21545
21548	22548	23548	24548	24547	22547	21547
21550	22550	23550	24550	24549	22549	21549
21552	22552	23552	24552	24551	22551	21551
21554	22554	23554	24554	24553	22553	21553
21556	22556	23556	24556	24555	22555	21555
21558	22558	23558	24558	24557	22557	21557
21560	22560	23560	24560	24559	22559	21559
21562	22562	23562	24562	24561	22561	21561
21564	22564	23564	24564	24563	22563	21563
21566	22566	23566	24566	24565	22565	21565

(D) Fitted with de-icing equipment.
*   Units temporary formed as 8 cars for short-term service Metropolitan Line:
21320-22320-25320-24320-24319-25382-22319-21319
21314-22324-25324-24324-24323-25384-22323-21323
21328-22328-25328-24328-24327-25386-22327-21327

DISTRICT LINE D STOCK

DM WEST LEADING	TRAILER	UNDM EAST MIDDLE	UNDM WEST MIDDLE	TRAILER	DM EAST LEADING		DM WEST LEADING	TRAILER	UNDM EAST MIDDLE	UNDM WEST MIDDLE	TRAILER	DM EAST LEADING
7000	17000(D)	8000	8001	17001	7001		7084	17084	8084	8085	17085	7085
7002	17002(D)	8002	8003	17003	7003		7086	17086	8086	8087	17087	7087
7004	17004(D)	8004	8005	17005	7005		7088	17088	8088	8089	17089	7089
7006	17006(D)	8006	8007	17007	7007		7090	17090	8090	8091	17091	7091
7008	17008(D)	8008	8009	17009	7009		7092	17092	8092	8093	17093	7093
7010	17010(D)	8010	8011	17011	7011		7094	17094	8094	8095	17095	7095
7012	17012(D)	8012	8013	17013	7013		7096	17096	8096	8097	17097	7097
7014	17014(D)	8014	8015	17015	7015		7098	17098	8098	8099	17099	7099
7016	17016(D)	8016	8017	17017	7017		7100	17100	8100	8101	17101	7101
7018	17018(D)	8018	8019	17019	7019		7102	17102	8102	8103	17103	7103
7020	17020(D)	8020	8021	17021	7021		7104	17104	8104	8105	17105	7105
7022	17022(D)	8022	8023	17023	7023		7106	17106	8106	8107	17107	7107
7024	17024(D)	8024	8025	17025	7025		7108	17108	8108	8109	17109	7109
7026	17026(D)	8026	8027	17027	7027		7110	17110	8110	8111	17111	7111
7028	17028(D)	8028	8029	17029	7029		7112	17112	8112	8113	17113	7113
7030	17030(D)	8030	8031	17031	7031		7114	17114	8114	8115	17115	7115
7032	17032(D)	8032	8033	17033	7033		7116	17116	8116	8117	17117	7117
7034	17034(D)	8034	8035	17035*	7035		7118	17118	8118	8119	17119	7119
7036	17036(D)	8036	8037	17037	7037		7120	17120	8120	8121	17121	7121
7038	17038(D)	8038	8039	17039	7039		7122	17122	8122	8123	17123	7123
7040	17040(D)	8040	8041	17041	7041		7124	17124	8124	8125	17125	7125
7042	17042(D)	8042	8043	17043	7043		7126	17126	8126	8127	17127	7127
7044	17044(D)	8044	8045	17045	7045		7128	17128	8128	8129	17129	7129
7046	17046(D)	8046	8047	17047	7047							
7048	17048(D)	8048	8049	17049	7049							
7050	17050	8050	8051	17051	7051							
7052	17052	8052	8053	17053	7053							
7054	17054	8054	8055	17055	7055							
7056	17056	8056	8057	17057	7057							
7058	17058	8058	8059	17059	7059							
7060	17060	8060	8061	17061	7061							
7062	17062	8062	8063	17063	7063							
7064	17064	8064	8065	17065	7065							
7066	17066	8066	8067	17067	7067							
7068	17068	8068	8069	17069	7069							
7070	17070	8070	8071	17071	7071							
7072	17072	8072	8073	17073	7073							
7074	17074	8074	8075	17075	7075							
7076	17076	8076	8077	17077*	7077							
7078	17078	8078	8079	17079	7079							
7080	17080	8080	8081	17081	7081							
7082	17082	8082	8083	17083	7083							

D STOCK DOUBLE-ENDED UNITS

DM WEST LEADING	TRAILER	UNDM EAST MIDDLE	UNDM WEST MIDDLE	TRAILER	DM EAST LEADING
7500	17500	7501	7520	17520	7521
7502	17502	7503	7522	17522	7523
7504	17504	7505	7524	17524	7525
7506	17506	7507	7526	17526	7527
7508	17508	7509	7528	17528	7529
7510	17510	7511	7530	17530	7531
7512	17512	7513	7532	17532	7533
7514	17514	7515	7534	17534	7535
7516	17516	7517	7536	17536	7537
7518	17518	7519	7538	17538	7539

* Trailers 17035 and 17077 were originally 17077 and 17035 respectively.

(D) Fitted with de-icing equipment.

C69/C77 STOCK: C69 Stock is the oldest stock in passenger service on the London Underground and, together with C77 Stock, is in course of replacement by the new S Stock during the currency of this book. Cars are numbered in the ranges 5501-5606 (C69 DMs) and 5701-5734 (C77 DMs) and 6501-6606 (C69 Trailers) and 6701-6734 (C77 DMs).

METROPOLITAN LINE S8 STOCK TRAINS

DM (A)	M1	M2	MS	MS	M2	M1	DM (D)		DM (A)	M1	M2	MS	MS	M2	M1	DM (D)
21002	22002	25002(D)	24002	24001	23001	22001	21001		21018	22018	25018(D)	24018	24017	23017	22017	21017
21004	22004	25004(D)	24004	24003	23003	22003	21003		21020	22020	25020(D)	24020	24019	23019	22019	21019
21006	22006	25006(D)	24006	24005	23005	22005	21005		21022	22022	25022(D)	24022	24021	23021	22021	21021
21008	22008	25008(D)	24008	24007	23007	22007	21007		21024	22024	25024(D)	24024	24023	23023	22023	21023
21010	22010	25010(D)	24010	24009	23009	22009	21009		21026	22026	25026(D)	24026	24025	23025	22025	21025
21012	22012	25012(D)	24012	24011	23011	22011	21011		21028	22028	25028(D)	24028	24027	23027	22027	21027
21014	22014	25014(D)	24014	24013	23013	22013	21013		21030	22030	25030(D)	24030	24029	23029	22029	21029
21016	22016	25016(D)	24016	24015	23015	22015	21015		21032	22032	25032(D)	24032	24031	23031	22031	21031

DM (A)	M1	M2	MS	MS	M2	M1	DM (D)
21034	22034	25034(D)	24034	24033	23033	22033	21033
21036	22036	25036(D)	24036	24035	23035	22035	21035
21038	22038	25038(D)	24038	24037	23037	22037	21037
21040	22040	25040(D)	24040	24039	23039	22039	21039
21042	22042	25042(D)	24042	24041	23041	22041	21041
21044	22044	25044(D)	24044	24043	23043	22043	21043
21046	22046	25046(D)	24046	24045	23045	22045	21045
21048	22048	25048(D)	24048	24047	23047	22047	21047
21050	22050	25050(D)	24050	24049	23049	22049	21049
21052	22052	25052(D)	24052	24051	23051	22051	21051
21054	22054	25054(D)	24054	24053	23053	22053	21053
21056	22056	25056(D)	24056	24055	23055	22055	21055
21058	22058	23058	24058	24057	23057	22057	21057
21060	22060	23060	24060	24059	23059	22059	21059
21062	22062	23062	24062	24061	23061	22061	21061
21064	22064	23064	24064	24063	23063	22063	21063
21066	22066	23066	24066	24065	23065	22065	21065
21068	22068	23068	24068	24067	23067	22067	21067
21070	22070	23070	24070	24069	23069	22069	21069
21072	22072	23072	24072	24071	23071	22071	21071
21074	22074	23074	24074	24073	23073	22073	21073
21076	22076	23076	24076	24075	23075	22075	21075
21078	22078	23078	24078	24077	23077	22077	21077
21080	22080	23080	24080	24079	23079	22079	21079
21082	22082	23082	24082	24081	23081	22081	21081
21084	22084	23084	24084	24083	23083	22083	21083
21086	22086	23086	24086	24085	23085	22085	21085
21088	22088	23088	24088	24087	23087	22087	21087
21090	22090	23090	24090	24089	23089	22089	21089
21092	22092	23092	24092	24091	23091	22091	21091
21094	22094	23094	24094	24093	23093	22093	21093
21096	22096	23096	24096	24095	23095	22095	21095
21098	22098	23098	24098	24097	23097	22097	21097
21100 *	22100	23100	24100	24099	23099	22099	21099
21102	22102	23102	24102	24101	23101	22101	21101
21104	22104	23104	24104	24103	23103	22103	21103
21106	22106	23106	24106	24105	23105	22105	21105
21108	22108	23108	24108	24107	23107	22107	21107
21110	22110	23110	24110	24109	23109	22109	21109
21112	22112	23112	24112	24111	23111	22111	21111
21114	22114	23114	24114	24113	23113	22113	21113
21116	22116	23116	24116	24115	23115	22115	21115

(D) Fitted with de-icing equipment.   * Named 'Tim O'Toole CBE'.

JUBILEE LINE 1996 TUBE STOCK

THREE-CAR 'A'-END UNITS			FOUR-CAR 'D'-END UNITS			
DM WEST/ NORTH	TRAILER	UNDM MIDDLE	UNDM MIDDLE	SPECIAL TRAILER	TRAILER	DM EAST/ SOUTH
96002	96202	96402	96401	96601	96201	96001
96004	96204	96404	96403	96603	96203	96003
96006	96206	96406	96405	96605	96205	96005
96008	96208	96408	96407	96607	96207	96007
96010	96210	96410	96409	96609	96209	96009
96012	96212	96412	96411	96611	96211	96011
96014	96214	96414	96413	96613	96213	96013
96016	96216	96416	96415	96615	96215	96015

(D) Fitted with de-icing equipment.

JUBILEE LINE 1996 TUBE STOCK

DM WEST/ NORTH	TRAILER	UNDM MIDDLE	UNDM MIDDLE	SPECIAL TRAILER	TRAILER	DM EAST/ SOUTH
96018	96218	96418	96417	96617	96217	96017
96020	96220	96420	96419	96619	96219	96019
96022	96222	96422	96421	96621	96221	96021
96024	96224	96424	96423	96623	96223	96023
96026	96226	96426	96425	96625	96225	96025
96028	96228	96428	96427	96627	96227	96027
96030	96230	96430	96429	96629	96229	96029
96032	96232	96432	96431	96631	96231	96031
96034	96234	96434	96433	96633	96233	96033
96036	96236	96436	96435	96635	96235	96035
96038	96238	96438	96437	96637	96237	96037
96040	96240	96440	96439	96639	96239	96039
96042	96242	96442	96441	96641	96241	96041
96044	96244	96444	96443	96643	96243	96043
96046	96246	96446	96445	96645	96245	96045
96048	96248	96448	96447	96647	96247	96047
96050	96250	96450	96449	96649	96249	96049
96052	96252	96452	96451	96651	96251	96051
96054	96254	96454	96453	96653	96253	96053
96056	96256	96456	96455	96655	96255	96055
96058	96258	96458	96457	96657	96257	96057
96060	96260	96460	96459	96659	96259	96059
96062	96262	96462	96461	96661	96261	96061
96064	96264	96464	96463	96663	96263	96063
96066	96266	96466	96465	96665	96265	96065
96068	96268	96468	96467	96667	96267	96067
96070	96270	96470	96469	96669	96269	96069
96072	96272	96472	96471	96671	96271	96071
96074	96274	96474	96473	96673	96273	96073
96076	96276	96476	96475	96675	96275	96075
96078	96278	96478	96477	96677	96277	96077
96080	96880(D)	96480	96479	96679	96279	96079
96082	96882(D)	96482	96481	96681	96281	96081
96084	96884(D)	96484	96483	96683	96283	96083
96086	96886(D)	96486	96485	96685	96285	96085
96088	96888(D)	96488	96487	96687	96287	96087
96090	96890(D)	96490	96489	96689	96289	96089
96092	96892(D)	96492	96491	96691	96291	96091
96094	96894(D)	96494	96493	96693	96293	96093
96096	96896(D)	96496	96495	96695	96295	96095
96098	96898(D)	96498	96497	96697	96297	96097
96100	96900(D)	96500	96499	96699	96299	96099
96102	96902(D)	96502	96501	96701	96301	96101
96104	96904(D)	96504	96503	96703	96303	96103
96106	96906(D)	96506	96505	96705	96305	96105
96108	96908(D)	96508	96507	96707	96307	96107
96110	96910(D)	96510	96509	96709	96309	96109
96112	96912(D)	96512	96511	96711	96311	96111
96114	96914(D)	96514	96513	96713	96313	96113
96116	96916(D)	96516	96515	96715	96315	96115
96118	96918(D)	96518	96517	96717	96317	96117
96120	96320	96520	96519	96719	96319	96119
96122	96322	96522	96521	96721	96321	96121
96124	96324	96524	96523	96723	96323	96123
96126	96326	96526	96525	96725	96325	96125

The last four trains in the list were additional trains delivered in 2005/06.
The Special Trailers were built and added to existing trains at the same time.

THREE-CAR 'D'-END UNITS

DM	TRAILER	UNDM MIDDLE
51501	52501	53501
51503	52503	53503
51505	52505	53505
51507	52507	53507
51509	52509	53509
51511	52511	53511
51513	52513	53513
51515	52515	53515
51517	52517	53517
51519	52519	53519
51521	52521	53521
51523	52523	53523
51525	52525	53525
51527	52527	53527
51529	52529	53529
51531	52531	53531
51533	52533	53533
51535	52535	53535
51537	52537	53537
51539	52539	53539
51541	52541	53541
51543	52543	53543
51545	52545	53545
51547	52547	53547
51549	52549	53549
51551	52551	53551
51553	52553	53553
51555	52555	53555
51557	52557	53557
51559	52559	53559
51561	52561	53561
51563	52563	53563
51565	52565	53565
51567	52567	53567
51569	52569	53569
51571	52571	53571
51573	52573	53573
51575	52575	53575
51577	52577	53577
51579	52579	53579
51581	52581	53581
51583	52583	53583
51585	52585	53585
51587	52587	53587
51589	52589	53589
51591	52591	53591
51593	52593	53593
51595	52595	53595
51597	52597	53597
51599	52599	53599
51601	52601	53601
51603	52603	53603
51605	52605	53605
51607	52607	53607
51609	52609	53609
51611	52611	53611

THREE-CAR 'A'-END UNITS

UNDM MIDDLE	TRAILER	DM
53502	52502	51502
53504	52504	51504
53506	52506	51506
53508	52508	51508
53510	52510	51510
53512	52512	51512
53514	52514	51514
53516	52516	51516
53518	52518	51518
53520	52520	51520
53522	52522	51522
53524	52524	51524
53526	52526	51526
53528	52528	51528
53530	52530	51530
53532	52532	51532
53534	52534	51534
53536	52536	51536
53538	52538	51538
53540	52540	51540
53542	52542	51542
53544	52544	51544
53546	52546	51546
53548	52548	51548
53550	52550	51550
53552	52552	51552
53554	52554	51554
53556	52556	51556
53558	52558	51558
53560	52560	51560
53562	52562	51562
53564	52564	51564
53566	52566	51566
53568	52568	51568
53570	52570	51570
53572	52572	51572
53574	52574	51574
53576	52576	51576
53578	52578	51578
53580	52580	51580
53582	52582	51582
53584	52584	51584
53586	52586	51586
53588	52588	51588
53590	52590	51590
53592	52592	51592
53594	52594	51594
53596	52596	51596
53598	52598	51598
53600	52600	51600
53602	52602	51602
53604	52604	51604
53606	52606	51606
53608	52608	51608
53610	52610	51610
53612	52612	51612

THREE-CAR 'D'-END UNITS

DM	TRAILER	UNDM MIDDLE
51613	52613	53613
51615	52615	53615
51617	52617	53617
51619	52619	53619
51621	52621	53621
51623	52623	53623
51625	52625	53625
51627	52627	53627
51629	52629	53629
51631	52631	53631
51633	52633	53633
51635	52635	53635
51637	52637	53637
51639	52639	53639
51641	52641	53641
51643	52643	53643
51645	52645	53645
51647	52647	53647
51649	52649	53649
51651	52651	53651
51653	52653	53653
51655	52655	53655
51657	52657	53657
51659	52659	53659
51661	52661	53661
51663	52663	53663
51665	52665	53665
51667	52667	53667
51669	52669	53669
51671	52671	53671
51673	52673	53673
51675	52675	53675
51677	52677	53677
51679	52679	53679
51681	52681	53681
51683	52683	53683
51685	52685	53685

THREE-CAR 'A'-END UNITS

UNDM MIDDLE	TRAILER	DM
53614	52614	51614
53616	52616	51616
53618	52618	51618
53620	52620	51620
53622	52622	51622
53624	52624	51624
53626	52626	51626
53628	52628	51628
53630	52630	51630
53632	52632	51632
53634	52634	51634
53636	52636	51636
53638	52638	51638
53640	52640	51640
53642	52642	51642
53644	52644	51644
53646	52646	51646
53648	52648	51648
53650	52650	51650
53652	52652	51652
53654	52654	51654
53656	52656	51656
53658	52658	51658
53660	52660	51660
53662	52662	51662
53664	52664	51664
53666	52666	51666
53668	52668	51668
53670	52670	51670
53672	52672	51672
53674	52674	51674
53676	52676	51676
53678	52678	51678
53680	52680	51680
53682	52682	51682
53684	52684	51684
53686	52686	51686

THREE-CAR 'D'-END DE-ICING UNITS

DM	DE-ICING TRAILER	UNDM MIDDLE
51701	52701	53701
51703	52703	53703
51705	52705	53705
51707	52707	53707
51709	52709	53709
51711	52711	53711
51713	52713	53713
51715	52715	53715
51717	52717	53717
51719	52719	53719
51721	52721	53721
51723	52723	53723
51725	52725	53725

THREE-CAR 'A'-END DE-ICING UNITS

UNDM MIDDLE	DE-ICING TRAILER	DM
53702	52702	51702
53704	52704	51704
53706	52706	51706
53708	52708	51708
53710	52710	51710
53712	52712	51712
53714	52714	51714
53716	52716	51716
53718	52718	51718
53720	52720	51720
53722	52722	51722
53724	52724	51724
53726	52726	51726

DM 'A'-END WEST LEADING	TRAILER	UNDM 'D'-END EAST MIDDLE	UNDM 'A'-END WEST MIDDLE	TRAILER	DM 'D'-END EAST LEADING
100	500	300	301	501	101
102	502	302	303	503	103
104	504	304	305	505	105
106	506	306	307	507	107
108	508	308	309	509	109
110	510	310	311	511	111
112	512	312	313	513	113
116	516	316	315	515	115
118	518	318	317	517	117
120	520	320	319	519	119
122	522	322	321	521	121
124	524	324	323	523	123
126	526	326	325	525	125
128	528	328	327	527	127
130	530	330	329	529	129
132	532	332	331	531	131
134	534	334	333	533	133
136	536	336	335	535	135
138	538	338	337	537	137
140	540	340	339	539	139
142	542	342	341	541	141
144	544	344	343	543	143
146	546	346	345	545	145
148	548	348	347	547	147
150	550	350	349	549	149
152	552	352	351	551	151
154	554	354	353	553	153
156	556	356	355	555	155
158	558	358	357	557	157
160	560	360	359	559	159
162	562	362	361	561	161
164	564	364	363	563	163
168	568	368	365	565	165
170	570	370	367	567	167
172	572	372	369	569	169
174	574	374	371	571	171
176	576	376	373	573	173
178	578	378	375	575	175
180	580	380	377	577	177
182	582	382	379	579	179
184	584	384	381	581	181
186	586	386	383	583	183
188	588	388	385	585	185
190	590	390	387	587	187
192	592	392	389	589	189
194	594	394	391	591	191
196	596	396	393	593	193
198	598	398	395	595	195

DM 'A'-END WEST LEADING	TRAILER	UNDM 'D'-END EAST MIDDLE	UNDM 'A'-END WEST MIDDLE	TRAILER	DM 'D'-END EAST LEADING
200	600	400	397	597	197
202	602	402	399	599	199
206	606(D)	406	401	601	201
208	608(D)	408	403	603	203
210	610(D)	410	405	605	205
212	612(D)	412	407	607	207
214	614(D)	414	409	609	209
216	616(D)	416	411	611	211
218	618(D)	418	413	613	213
220	620(D)	420	415	615	215
222	622(D)	422	417	617	217
224	624(D)	424	419	619	219
226	626(D)	426	421	621	221
228	628(D)	428	423	623	223
230	630(D)	430	425	625	225
232	632(D)	432	427	627	227
234	634(D)	434	429	629	229
236	636(D)	436	431	631	231
238	638(D)	438	433	633	233
240	640(D)	440	435	635	235
242	642(D)	442	437	637	237
244	644(D)	444	439	639	239
246	644(D)	446	441	641	241
248	648(D)	448	443	643	243
250	650(D)	450	445	645	245
252	652(D)	452	447	647	247
			449	649	249
			451	651	251
			453	653	253

DOUBLE-ENDED UNITS

DM 'A'-END WEST	TRAILER	DM 'D'-END EAST	DM 'A'-END WEST	TRAILER	DM 'D'-END EAST
854	654	855	876	676	877
856	656	857	878	678	879
858	658	859	880	680	881
860	660	861	882	682	883
862	662	863	884	684	885
864	664	865	886	686	887
866	666	867	890	690	891
868	668	869	892	692	893
870	670	871	894	694	895
872	672	873	896*	696*	897*
874	674	875			

*   Cars renumbered ex 114-688-889 respectively.
(D) Fitted with de-icing equipment.

VICTORIA LINE 2009 TUBE STOCK

A1 DM	B1 TRAILER	C1 NDM	D1 UNDM	D UNDM	C NDM	B TRAILER	A DM
11002	12002	13002	14002	14001	13001	12001	11001
11004	12004	13004	14004	14003	13003	12003	11003
11006	12006	13006	14006	14005	13005	12005	11005
11008	12008	13008	14008	14007	13007	12007	11007
11010	12010	13010	14010	14009	13009	12009	11009
11012	12012	13012	14012	14011	13011	12011	11011
11014	12014	13014	14014	14013	13013	12013	11013
11016	12016	13016	14016	14015	13015	12015	11015
11018	12018	13018	14018	14017	13017	12017	11017
11020	12020	13020	14020	14019	13019	12019	11019
11022	12022	13022	14022	14021	13021	12021	11021
11024	12024	13024	14024	14023	13023	12023	11023
11026	12026	13026	14026	14025	13025	12025	11025
11028	12028	13028	14028	14027	13027	12027	11027
11030	12030	13030	14030	14029	13029	12029	11029
11032	12032	13032	14032	14031	13031	12031	11031
11034	12034	13034	14034	14033	13033	12033	11033
11036	12036	13036	14036	14035	13035	12035	11035
11038	12038	13038	14038	14037	13037	12037	11037
11040	12040	13040	14040	14039	13039	12039	11039
11042	12042	13042	14042	14041	13041	12041	11041
11044	12044	13044	14044	14043	13043	12043	11043
11046	12046	13046	14046	14045	13045	12045	11045
11048	12048	13048	14048	14047	13047	12047	11047

A1 DM	B1 TRAILER	C1 NDM	D1 UNDM	D UNDM	C NDM	B TRAILER	A DM
11050	12050	13050	14050	14049	13049	12049	11049
11052	12052	13052	14052	14051	13051	12051	11051
11054	12054	13054	14054	14053	13053	12053	11053
11056	12056	13056	14056	14055	13055	12055	11055
11058	12058	13058	14058	14057	13057	12057	11057
11060	12060	13060	14060	14059	13059	12059	11059
11062	12062	13062	14062	14061	13061	12061	11061
11064	12064	13064	14064	14063	13063	12063	11063
11066	12066	13066	14066	14065	13065	12065	11065
11068	12068	13068	14068	14067	13067	12067	11067
11070	12070	13070	14070	14069	13069	12069	11069
11072	12072	13072	14072	14071	13071	12071	11071
11074	12074	13074	14074	14073	13073	12073	11073
11076	12076	13076	14076	14075	13075	12075	11075
11078	12078	13078	14078	14077	13077	12077	11077
11080	12080	13080	14080	14079	13079	12079	11079
11082	12082	13082	14082	14081	13081	12081	11081
11084	12084	13084	14084	14083	13083	12083	11083
11086	12086	13086	14086	14085	13085	12085	11085
11088	12088	13088	14088	14087	13087	12087	11087
11090	12090	13090	14090	14089	13089	12089	11089
11092	12092	13092	14092	14091	13091	12091	11091
11094	12094	13094	14094	14093	13093	12093	11093

WATERLOO & CITY LINE
1992 TUBE STOCK TWO-CAR 'E' - 'F' UNITS

DM	NDM	DM	NDM	DM	NDM	DM	NDM
65501	67501	65504	67504	65507	67507	65510	67510
65502	67502	65505	67505	65508	67508		
65503	67503	65506	67506	65509	67509		

OVERGROUND CLASS 172

UNIT No.	DMSO	DMSO
172001	59311	59411
172002	59312	59412
172003	59313	59413
172004	59314	59414
172005	59315	59415
172006	59316	59416
172007	59317	59417
172008	59318	59418

OVERGROUND CLASS 378/1

UNIT No.	DMSO	MSO	TSO	DMSO
378135	38035	38235	38335	38135
378136	38036	38236	38336	38136
378137	38037	38237	38337	38137
378138	38038	38238	38338	38138
378139	38039	38239	38339	38139
378140	38040	38240	38340	38140
378141	38041	38241	38341	38141
378142	38042	38242	38342	38142
378143	38043	38243	38343	38143
378144	38044	38244	38344	38144
378145	38045	38245	38345	38145
378146	38046	38246	38346	38146
378147	38047	38247	38347	38147
378148	38048	38248	38348	38148
378149	38049	38249	38349	38149
378150 (D)	38050	38250	38350	38150
378151 (D)	38051	38251	38351	38151
378152 (D)	38052	38252	38352	38152
378153 (D)	38053	38253	38353	38153
378154 (D)	38054	38254	38354	38154

(D)   Fitted with de-icing equipment

OVERGROUND CLASS 378/2

UNIT No.	DMSO	MSO	PTSO	DMSO
378201	38001	38201	38301	38101
378202	38002	38202	38302	38102
378203	38003	38203	38303	38103
378204	38004	38204	38304	38104
378205	38005	38205	38305	38105
378206	38006	38206	38306	38106
378207	38007	38207	38307	38107
378208	38008	38208	38308	38108
378209	38009	38209	38309	38109
378210	38010	38210	38310	38110
378211	38011	38211	38311	38111
378212	38012	38212	38312	38112
378213	38013	38213	38313	38113
378214	38014	38214	38314	38114
378215	38015	38215	38315	38115
378216 (D)	38016	38216	38316	38116
378217 (D)	38017	38217	38317	38117
378218 (D)	38018	38218	38318	38118
378219 (D)	38019	38219	38319	38119
378220 (D)	38020	38220	38320	38120
378221	38021	38221	38321	38121
378222	38022	38222	38322	38122
378223	38023	38223	38323	38123
378224	38024	38224	38324	38124
378225	38025	38225	38325	38125
378226	38026	38226	38326	38126
378227	38027	38227	38327	38127
378228	38028	38228	38328	38128
378229	38029	38229	38329	38129
378230	38030	38230	38330	38130
378231	38031	38231	38331	38131
378232	38032	38232	38332	38132
378233	38033	38233	38333	38133
378234	38034	38234	38334	38134
378255	38055	38255	38355	38155
378256	38056	38256	38356	38156
378257	38057	38257	38357	38157

(D)   Fitted with de-icing equipment

OVERGROUND TRAIN STABLING (excluding spares)

North London Line*	Willesden	Euston	Stratford	Richmond	Watford	Camden
Total trains: 26	6	9	3	3	3	2

East London Line	New Cross Gate	Crystal Palace	Clapham Junction
Total trains: 27	20	4	3

Goblin Line	Barking
Total trains: 8	8

*   Includes West London Line

UNDERGROUND TRAIN STABLING (excluding spares)

	BAKERLOO		CENTRAL		NORTHERN	
Main Depots	Stonebridge Park	13	Ruislip	17	Golders Green	16
Subsidiary Depots	Queen's Park	7	Hainault	33	Morden	38
Sidings	London Road	10	White City	11	Edgware	13
	Elephant & Castle	2	Loughton	10	High Barnet	8
			Woodford	6	Highgate	16
Platform	Elephant & Castle	1				
Totals		**33**		**77**		**91**

	PICCADILLY		VICTORIA		JUBILEE	
Main Depots	Northfields	33	Northumberland Park	31	Stratford Market	27
Subsidiary Depots	Cockfosters	34			Neasden	20
Sidings	Arnos Grove	6	Brixton	2	Stanmore	10
	South Harrow	4	Victoria	1		
	Acton Town	1	Walthamstow	2		
Platform	Uxbridge	1				
Totals		**79**		**36**		**57**

	DISTRICT		CIRCLE/H&C		METROPOLITAN	
Main Depots	Ealing Common	23	Hammersmith	8	Neasden	26
Subsidiary Depots	Upminster	32				
Minor Depots	Lillie Bridge	7	Lillie Bridge	2		
	Hammersmith	2				
Sidings	Parsons Green	8	Farringdon	1	Rickmansworth	9
	Barking	1	Barking	12	Uxbridge	11
	Triangle Sidings	1	Triangle Sidings	2	Watford	3
Platforms	High Street Kensington	1	Edgware Road	2	Watford	1
	Richmond	1	Hammersmith	2		
			Moorgate	2		
			Aldgate	1		
Totals		**76**		**32**		**50**

	WATERLOO & CITY	
Main Depots	Waterloo	4
Platform	Bank	1
Totals		**5**

APPENDIX: Technical Terms

Automatic Train Operation (ATO) and **Automatic Train Protection (ATP)**.
ATO is essentially an automatic driving mechanism that controls the starting, stopping acceleration and deceleration of the train. It requires a 'train attendant' to be on board, principally for dealing with incidents and to drive the train manually if the automatic system fails. By contrast, ATP provides the train driver with an additional reminder of signal aspects and enforces a stop signal if ignored. Although separate functions, ATO and ATP frequently are installed together, as happened in September 1968 when the Victoria Line became the first fully automatic passenger carrying railway in the world.

Deadman (vigilance) device. Passenger safety depends on action being taken if a train operator becomes incapacitated, which is what this device achieves by requiring the operator to release a switch momentarily and re-apply it at timed intervals. If the operator fails to carry out this function (or ignores visual and audible warnings) the train's brakes are applied automatically.

Driverless Train Operation (DTO). DTO is one step advanced from ATO, with no driver but retaining a member of staff on the train. The trains on the Docklands Light Railway employ DTO.

Dual-system. In the context of electric trains this means a motor car that can operate on both third-rail DC and overhead line AC electrification systems.

Insulated Gate Bipolar Transistor. The IGBT is a type of electronic switch used for controlling motors and other electrical devices. On electric trains it enables operators to achieve the efficiency advantages of an AC three-phase motor even though this is being driven from a DC supply.

Regenerative braking. A system of dynamic braking in which direct-current drive motors are used as generators. Kinetic energy is converted into electrical energy that is returned to the conductor rails. Regenerative braking can deliver a considerable saving in electrical energy.

Rheostatic braking. A system of dynamic braking in which direct-current drive motors are used as generators. Kinetic energy is converted into electrical energy that is then dissipated as heat in a braking rheostat connected to the motor armature. In this case the electrical energy produced is lost as heat.

Unattended Train Operation (UTO). UTO, in service on the Meteor Line in Paris since 1998, exploits driverless trains with no member of staff aboard for controlling the trains. This relies on infrastructure systems that know precisely where every train is and how fast it is travelling. The system can be capable of self-optimisation to meet differing goals for different trains at different times of the day. UTO is expected to become commonplace on metros in future.